E99.C5K49   WITHDRAWN

15.00

D1204142

WALK IN YOUR SOUL

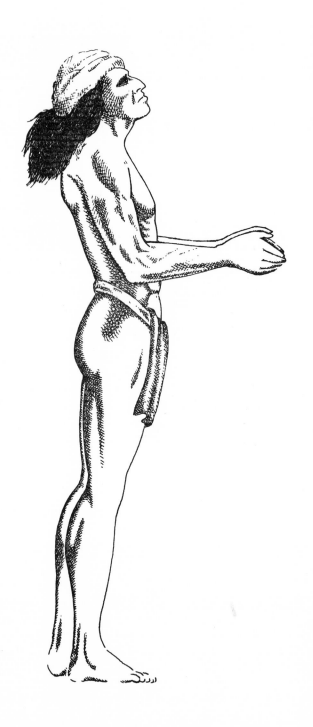

WALK IN YOUR SOUL

Love Incantations of the Oklahoma Cherokees

JACK FREDERICK KILPATRICK
ANNA GRITTS KILPATRICK

SOUTHERN METHODIST UNIVERSITY PRESS : DALLAS

© 1965 : SOUTHERN METHODIST UNIVERSITY PRESS : DALLAS

LIBRARY OF CONGRESS CATALOGUE CARD NUMBER : 65-24931

Illustrations by William D. Wittliff

ACKNOWLEDGMENTS

All translations that appear in this volume are from documents in the personal collection of the authors. All Cherokee terms are rendered in LK, the orthographic system for writing Cherokee with roman letters designed for the Smithsonian Institution by Professor Floyd G. Lounsbury of Yale University and the senior author of the present volume.

The authors acknowledge with gratitude that certain phases of the research necessary for the preparation of this book were made possible by the financial support of the National Science Foundation.

They also wish to express their thanks to Mrs. Benjamin A. Petty for the typing of the manuscript of the book.

JACK FREDERICK KILPATRICK
ANNA GRITTS KILPATRICK

CONTENTS

>>>

WALK IN YOUR SOUL

INTRODUCTION

IT IS NOT surprising that the erotic magic of the Oklahoma Cherokees has remained little known; for it has held out small promise to investigators. The best potential informant upon it, the fullblood layman, knows very little of it, almost certainly far less than his ancestors knew; the Space Age medicine man is no more communicative than were his guildsmen of yore; the educated mixed-blood knows of it merely by hearsay. A very small amount of it that has been written down in Sequoyah syllabary has found its way into the collections of museums and libraries, and even were any sizable body of it available to scholarship, proficiency in ritualistic Cherokee apparently is not.

In view of the fact that to our knowledge sociological studies pertinent to the problem do not exist, one can arrive at no acceptable appraisal of the viability of erotic magic in the society of the Oklahoma Cherokees today. Beyond saying that for a certainty it is still employed, and that probably it is used to a very limited extent, it would be hazardous to go.

All indications point to there having existed up until a generation ago hundreds of erotic charms in manuscripts in the possession of both the laity and medicine men, but chiefly, of course, in the hands of the latter. The dramatic acceleration in acculturation resulting from World War II and the postwar social order has been devastating to

Cherokee manuscript materials. One may merely glean these days, not harvest.

Oklahoma Cherokee erotic magic has been found inscribed in huge ledgers, in pocket notebooks, and upon loose sheets of paper varying from folio to not much larger than a postage stamp in size. Business account books and grocery lists are enlivened with incantations for making a woman lovesick, and staid family records are spiced with information on how to "rebeautify" oneself. In short, erotic magic is likely to be found written wherever its writer discovered a bit of white space. And since any manuscript in which it appears is likely to be at least a generation old, it will almost certainly be grievously torn, stained, or blurred; and moreover, inasmuch as the Cherokee people at no time numbered among their many virtues an irreproachability in spelling, the orthography in that manuscript is apt to be adventurous to the point of recklessness.

2.

"Sacred formulas," the term confected by James Mooney three-quarters of a century ago for the religious, medical, and magical texts of the Cherokees, is in many respects a fitting one, but it fails to catch the spirit of Cherokee thought. The word "formula" possesses connotations of rigidity that dissonate clangorously with an ineradicable inherent plasticity in the practice of Cherokee magic, and certainly, within the accepted meaning of the term, many of the "formulas" are far from "sacred." The Cherokee designation for one of their texts, *i:gawé:sdi*, is a far more meaningful term; for most Cherokee magical rituals consist of something that one says (or merely thinks) or sings, called the *i:gawé:sdi* ("to say, one"), and some recommended physical procedures, called the *igv́:n(e)dhi* ("to do, one"), although some have no *igv́:n(e)dhi* at all. The published literature on Cherokee magic does not recognize a fundamental truth: in any magical ritual all generative power resides in thought, and the *i:gawé:sdi*, which focuses and directs that thought, alone is inviolate. The *igv́:n(e)dhi*, which merely augments the authority of thought, or serves more effectively to apply or disseminate it, may be expanded, curtailed, altered, or dispensed with entirely in conformity with personal preference, special circumstances, or the broad general principles that govern Cherokee medico-religious practice.

There are striking parallels between the Cherokee magical ritual and the Roman Catholic Mass. An *i:gawé:sdi* may have its Ordinary and Proper aspects; and just as we have the *Missa solemnis* and the *Missa lecta*, so do we have Cherokee texts that may optionally be sung or spoken. And while it is true that the Cherokee shaman is no more at liberty to alter phraseology than is the celebrant of the Eucharist, certain interpolations, analogous to the tropes of the Middle Ages, are admissible.

Most commonly these extraneous elements take the form of: the repetition of a key word the sacred four times; the interjection of the supremely sacrosanct numeral seven; the insertion of the pronoun *ayv* ("I"); and a hiatus in which the reciter thinks intently upon the purpose of the ritual. These are not introduced with complete freedom, but only at certain junctures approved by custom, and they are usually indicated in manuscript texts by symbols—crosses, numerals, a series of vertical dashes, and the like.

From the published literature one might get the impression that a particular *i:gawé:sdi* is usable for but one highly specific purpose, whereas in reality any *i:gawé:sdi* is serviceable for any number of purposes for which its wording qualifies it.

A love incantation may bear a caption delineating its purpose plus a subscript sentence or two prescribing (not categorically dictating) an implementation of the charm; but there are numerous *idi:gawé:sdi* (the plural of *i:gawé:sdi*) for which one or the other, or even both, may be lacking, and sometimes all information pertinent to an example is written at its beginning or its end.

The opening of an *i:gawé:sdi* typically incorporates one or more of the following formalized elements: a device to command attention, "Now!" or "Now! Listen!"; the name of the spirit petitioned plus his ritualistic color which relates to the role that he is to play; an identification of the place of residence of the spirit; an assurance that the powers of the spirit are limitless; a statement to the effect that with dispatch the spirit has already arrived to give ear to a request. If all of these components were present, the stereotype would present this appearance:

> Now! Listen!
> Red Raven!
> Your Place of Peace is Above.
> You are a Great Wizard.
> You fail in nothing.
> Quickly You have just come to hear.

The North Carolina Cherokee love incantations translated by Mooney ("Sacred Formulas of the Cherokees," in *Seventh Annual Report*, Bureau of American Ethnology, pp. 375-84), despite damaging inaccuracies, are exceedingly beautiful; but the fashion in which they are arranged on the printed page does violence to the basic structure of the Cherokee *i:gawé:sdi*. A rearrangement by Astrov (*American Indian Prose and Poetry*, pp. 175-77) of one of these texts follows Mooney's precedent.

Neither Mooney nor Astrov perceived that the demands of sacred numerology are fully met in the Cherokee *i:gawé:sdi* and that a translation of it must preserve that fulfilment. Anyone who can read Cherokee can readily see that religious, medical, and magical texts are built upon patterns that take full advantage of the powers resident in the minor sacred numeral four or major sacred numeral seven. This accession to numerological fiat usually results in a given text's being structured into four or seven lines, into four or seven groups of lines, or into major divisions subdivided into units of four or seven.

There are certain phraseological ritualisms that are liberally strewn throughout all Cherokee magic. Every action transpires "quickly" or "very quickly," and the force of that action is exerted in the "middle" or the "very middle" of its recipient. The interjection "Ha!" heard almost not at all in daily speech, and the "Seven Clans" and the "Seven Clan Districts" are to be seen very frequently, as are various imitations of thunderclaps and lightning flashes. There is much "climbing over" and "going under," and no little alluding to "Pathways," both "White" and "Blue." The "Now, one assumes!" has something of the same force as "So be it!"

>>>

The seven colors of Cherokee magical symbolism are
associated with both compass points and qualities:

Red—East—Victory, power.

Blue—North—Failure, weakness, spiritual depression.

Black—West—Death, oblivion.

White—South—Happiness, peace.

Brown—Normality, the earth.

Purple—Witchcraft, evil.

Yellow—A sinister influence, or power.

The color symbolism that we discover in both the
magic and the medicine is exceedingly subtle. In a broad
sense colors are affiliated with directions and stylized attributes, but the incantator applies his colors like a painter in
order to produce a total impression, and with his palette
he can make a thought painting gradually glow, or fade
into sepulchral and sinister purples, blues, and blacks.
Through colors he achieves dramatic development.

Erotic incantations are either merely said (or sung, or
thought), or else used to infuse tobacco with magical
powers—to "remake" it. Some *idi:gawé:sdi* are employed in
both fashions. In a tobacco-"remaking" ritual commercial
tobacco is ordinarily used, but sometimes *tso:lagayv̇:li*
(*Nicotina rustica*) is substituted for it. The use of the latter
is socially condemned; for its potency is held to be limitless and dangerous to the life of a woman.

While tobacco can theoretically be "remade" at any
time, in any place, its power is greatly augmented by its
being prepared while facing east at dawn by flowing water.

3.

The word *ada:wé:hi*—which we, like Mooney and like

Olbrechts, for want of a more nearly exact term translate as "Wizard"—appears in Cherokee *idi:gawé:sdi* with an almost predictable frequency. And with a frequency that is depressingly predictable, in white men's books about the Cherokees the term is equated with *medicine man*. The chances of the average Roman Catholic priest for achieving canonization are far greater than those of a Cherokee medicine man for ever being considered to be an *ada:wé:hi*; for an *ada:wé:hi* is a being, spiritual or human, of boundless powers. And the Cherokee traditionalist passes anew over the Trail of Tears at perceiving upon the printed page *adawehis* standing as a plural. His dismay is no less than that of the English purist when brought up short with "ten sheeps" or a "pair of deers." The plural of *ada:wé:hi* is *ani:da:wé:hi*.

The correct term for a Cherokee shaman who, like the Jewish rabbi, is both physician and priest, is *dida:hnvwi:-sg(i)* ("curer of them, he"). His antitype, the individual who unauthorizedly uses knowledge for evil ends, is a *dida:hnese:sg(i)* ("putter-in and drawer-out of them, he")—a sorcerer, a "witch." Any *dida:hnvwi:sg(i)* knows everything a *dida:hnese:sg(i)* knows, and even more; but he uses his knowledge in a selfless and socially sanctioned way to counter and to crush evil.

The Cherokee medicine man—typically a kindly, helpful, and humble servant of his people—is traditionally, among many other things, a marriage counselor and an adviser to the lovelorn. A young man has a problem: his perfectly legitimate suit for the hand of a young lady goes on square wheels. The lover places his despair in the able hands of the medicine man, who teaches him a little ritual

>>>

which produces results that no woman can resist. A girl
has a similar problem: the young man of her fancy dallies
along the road to matrimony. All she needs is a little spell
to "rebeautify" herself, and the laggard becomes a man of
action. A young husband is distressed no end at the ten-
dency of his wife to belittle his bed and board by casting
backward glances at home and mother. His mind can be
put at ease forthwith. The medicine man knows magic of
such potency as to make a two-room cabin appear posi-
tively palatial. A wife is distraught; her heretofore staid
mate has developed a weakness for the charms of an un-
attached, and perhaps unattachable, young woman. She
needs, and gets, a spiritual sledgehammer which is certain
to break up the scandalous liaison that mars her matri-
monial bliss.

4.

The majority of the erotic magical texts carry some general identification such as *anige:hyv ugv:wahli* ("women,
for the purpose of"); and whereas in some instances some
nonspecific designation such as this may be applied to
charms that actually have a more restricted purpose, in
most cases such a labeling is quite appropriate: a certain
charm will be for attracting the affections of an individual
female, or perhaps womanhood in general. "Attraction"
idi:gawé:sdi may be of either the sung or spoken type; they
may be merely said or sung, used in "going to the water"
(see Mooney, "The Cherokee River Cult," in *Journal of
American Folklore*, XIII, 1-10, *passim*), or employed in
"remaking" tobacco.

Although we have consistently translated the term *uhí:-*

soʔdí as "lonely" or "loneliness," in reality it is an exceedingly difficult word to define. Mooney ("Sacred Formulas," p. 377) observes that it is "... a very expressive word to a Cherokee and is of constant recurrence in the love formulas. It refers to that intangible something characteristic of certain persons which inevitably chills and depresses the spirits of all who may be so unfortunate as to come within its influences." The authors point out (*Friends of Thunder,* p. 191) that it is "... a state of ecstatic yearning, an otherworldly melancholia peculiarly Cherokeean. It is generally attributed to the sorcery of an enemy."

A subtype of the attraction charm is the incantation to produce *uhí:soʔdí* in a woman. The excruciating lovesickness that results from the use of such magic causes a woman to be repelled by her familiar associations and surroundings, and drives her to seek surcease in the arms of her enchanter. Several North Carolina *uhí:soʔdí*-producing *idi:-gawé:sdi* are recorded in Mooney ("Sacred Formulas," pp. 375-80). Like other "attraction" incantations, they may be either said or sung, employed in "going to the water," or utilized in tobacco "remaking."

Those incantations called *ado:dhlvhi:soʔdí:yi* ("to 'remake' oneself"), together with a subspecies of them known as *ado:du:hisoʔdí:yi* ("to 'rebeautify' oneself"), form one of the largest bodies of erotic *idi:gawé:sdi*. A person who has "remade" himself has surrounded the ego with a spiritual aura through which the light of the old self is brilliantly refracted. It is obvious that in the popular mind the difference between "to 'remake' oneself" and "to 'rebeautify' oneself" lies in the greater emphasis that the latter lends to physical attractiveness as contrasted with spiritual attractiveness. The practical results of both are held to be very nearly identical.

One gets the impression that the typical *ado:dhlvhi:-soʔdi:yi* or *ado:du:hisoʔdi:yi* is recited (or sung) as circumstances dictate, although it can be used for "going to the water," and individual examples of this genre specifically prescribe this procedure. Tobacco is not employed in "remaking oneself" or in "rebeautifying oneself."

There is an entire class of incantations that, to our knowledge, has not been reported. While specimens in this category are captioned variously—"If a woman scorns one" and "If a woman pretends to be superior" are representative labels—the purpose of them all is the same: to lower the self-esteem of a haughty, coquettish, or faultfinding girl friend or wife. These woman-taming spells, some of which are used in tobacco-preparing, are quite distinct from the type mentioned by Mooney and Olbrechts (*The Swimmer Manuscript,* p. 155) for making a woman unattractive to men.

Gala:n(i)sdoʔdi ("to acclimate one with, one") incantations are distantly related to the foregoing ones, but the primary purpose of a *gala:n(i)sdoʔdi,* palest of all white magic, is to assist a bride in accepting her new surroundings. With "to acclimate" incantations sometimes tobacco is used and sometimes it is not; in any event, the motive of the incantator is of the noblest. The two exceedingly beautiful North Carolina incantations reported by Mooney ("Sacred Formulas," pp. 380-81, 383-84) are *gala:n(i)-sdoʔdi.*

In the van of all evil incantations are those known as *di:dagale:n(v)dhoʔdi:yi* ("to separate them with, one"), spells that break up friendships and marriages. For the most part *di:dagale:n(v)dho?dí:yi* magic is resorted to by a disgruntled suitor who has lost a love match, but sometimes it is used to achieve revenge for any sort of wrong. Occasionally it is employed by a *dida:hnvwi:sg(i)* to smash the intrigues of a pair of mates or a coalition of friends who seek to injure him or one of his clients. The power of this sorcery is fearful indeed: for it can do anything from fomenting a quarrel to taking human life. Most "to separate" spells are for "remaking" tobacco, but some need merely be said, or thought.

A good many erotic *idi:gawé:sdi* apply to very specific problems. Some are for "remaking" a comb, so that its user may fix the focus of attractiveness in the coiffure. Some without rancor quietly take away from one who is a rival, but not an enemy, a lover or mate. There are those to make a man or woman preternaturally unattractive to a roving eye, and there are those to placate the anger of a sweetheart or wife. One can counter the machinations of the covetous, and one can compel a runaway spouse to return home.

It is the unhappy duty of the authors to point out that for any Cherokee erotic *i:gawé:sdi* to possess even the slightest degree of utility it must be delivered in Cherokee.

I
ATTRACTING

I

ATTRACTING

1.

Now! Then this, ⸺⸺⸺, is your name, you woman,
and you think of my body, which is not to be forgot-
ten!

I am named ⸺⸺⸺.

Cherokees as a whole do not believe that there is any
inherent relationship between the length of a conjuration
or incantation and its power: either a specific text is forceful or it is not. Indeed, we have heard a medicine man
express himself to the effect that he had a decided personal preference toward brief *idi:gawé:sdi,* and that many
items in his repertoire were, in his opinion, needlessly ver-
bose. However, a specimen of a love incantation as brief
as the above is to be encountered but rarely.

Although this charm bears no caption and no accompanying directions, it is obvious that its purpose is to capture the affections of a specific individual. It is the sort of
magic that is handed down for generation after generation
in the laity. Undoubtedly, one merely says it the regula-
tion four times, and probably blows the breath toward or
upon the target individual after each recitation.

The term "you woman" does not have in Cherokee the
same flavor that it has in English. In the latter language it
carries a somewhat denigrating connotation; it smacks of

"the Jones woman" designation beloved by reporters on the city desk whose news stories deal with arrests for soliciting and disturbing the peace of the other side of the tracks. "You man" or "you woman" rings with human dignity in the language of a people to whom the attainment of maturity is a noble fulfilment of nature, worthy of all honor. One is tempted to translate "you woman" as "Madam," or perhaps "Lady."

The above charm came from *Gi:dhahyó:hi*, the Cherokee community that lies in a wide and beautiful valley a few miles south of Stilwell, the county seat of Adair County.

2.

Now!
Ha, then! You women of the Seven Clans!

Ha! Now it has surely become time!

All of you have just come to put White Eyes into me.

Ha, then! All of you will not be able to glance elsewhere. It will be my body alone upon which all of you will be gazing!

The *"Gha?!"* with which the majority of Oklahoma Cherokee conjurations and incantations begin is an interjection that could be translated in a number of ways— "Attention!" or "Hear this!" or "Well!" for example—but "Now!" appears to us to be the most appropriate rendering. It is not a ritualism; it is generously employed in workaday writing and conversation for the purpose of prefacing a new thought.

The Cherokee people aboriginally were segmented into seven matrilineal exogamous "clans" called *Ani:wahhya, Ani:saho:ni, Ani:gilo:hi, Ani:wo:di, Ani:tsi:sghwa, Ani:gha:- wi,* and *Ani:godage:wi.* While the meanings of some of these clan designations are obvious, the etymologies of others stand in need of study. Some of them are mistranslated, without exception, in every standard bibliographic source. The term *Ani:gilo:hi,* for example, is invariably rendered "Twisters," or "Long Hairs." The Cherokees, with a depressing lack of respect for the advanced degrees of anthropologists, stubbornly insist that the name of the clan is something to the effect of "They just became offended" (see Kilpatrick, "An Etymological Note . . . ," *Journal of the Graduate Research Center,* XXX, 41). The *Ani:saho:ni,* says academic authority, are the "Blue" people. The "Blue" people, deprived of the advantages of summer field trips to the Cherokees, go right on believing that their clan name was derived from that of a large extinct feline.

In Cherokee magic the terms "Seven Clans" and "Seven Clan Districts" are commonly employed as figures of speech to signify the whole of the Cherokee people, and are sometimes used as a symbol for the entire world. They equate, to some degree, with the "Seven Seas" and the "Six Continents" clichés in English.

Cherokee, one of the most transcendentally complex systems of communication ever devised by man, abounds in verb-forms of which there are no real equivalents in the comparatively simple Indo-European languages. Of one of these James Mooney, the most inspired scholar who ever studied the Cherokees, has this to say in reference to his pioneer translations of North Carolina Cherokee *idi:gawé:-sdi*:

> On examining the text the student cannot fail to be struck by the great number of verbs ending in *iga*. This is a peculiar form hardly ever used excepting in these formulas [*idi:gawé:sdi*], where almost every paragraph contains one or more such verbs. It implies that the subject has just come and is now performing the action, and that he came for that purpose (*Sacred Formulas*, p. 344).

"All of you have just come to put . . . into me," a single word in Cherokee, is one of the *-iga* verb-forms.

In the symbolism of the magical *idi:gawé:sdi* the putting of "White Eyes" into the body of an individual is the looking upon that person with desire, favor, or goodwill by those of the opposite sex.

The brief direction appended to this incantation from *Gwagwó:hi* on the left bank of upper Tenkiller Lake in Cherokee County informs us that the charm is merely to be said. It is the type of *i:gawé:sdi* that a young man might use before attending a gathering at which girls would be present.

3.

Now! I am as beautiful as the Carolina Wren!

All of you women, I have just come to touch you!

All of you, then, have just come to put White Eyes into my body.

≺≺≺

All of you will be gazing at me alone.

I have just come to touch all of you White Women!

The Carolina wren (*Thryothorus ludovicianus*) is seldom mentioned in *idi:gawé:sdi*. One wonders why this rather plain bird is here held up as a paragon of loveliness, although, to be sure, it is graceful and agile on the wing.

The Cherokee language, fantastically rich in verbs, is adjectivally rather poor. That which in English might be described as "handsome," "lovely," or "winsome," would be obdurately "beautiful" in Cherokee. One might question the appropriateness of "beautiful" as applied to a male, but one must remember that a proper incantation confers preternatural benefits. Oddly enough, in Cherokee the verb "to touch" has, just as in English, the force of arousing the emotions in addition to tactile connotations.

Needless to say, the "White Women" in the incantation are not Caucasians; "White" ritualistically signifies the highest degree of desirability.

We are unable to say from what community this charm, captioned "For women. To say four times," came. It was written in a copy, made recently at *Gwagwó:hi,* of some other, older medicine book. As in the case of No. 2, its chief usefulness is in preparing for attending gatherings where girls are among those gathered.

4.

Now! Listen!
Black Yellow Mockingbird!

>>

Very quickly You have just come down to the very middle
  of her soul.
(This is her name: _____, and her people are _____.)

Now quickly my footprints have just come to meet the
  White Pathways that lie before her!

(My people are _____.)

We have followed the precedent established by Mooney
("Sacred Formulas," pp. 345-97, *passim*) in translating the
attention-getting interjection "*Sge?!*" as "Listen!"

That bird spirit, the Yellow Mockingbird (yellow-
breasted chat, *Icteria virens virens*), flits ubiquitously
through Cherokee erotic magic. He is also petitioned in
sorcery for the purpose of obtaining wealth and the guard-
ing of a house. The Yellow Mockingbird (*huhu* in Cherokee) marries a girl in a North Carolina Cherokee myth
recorded by Mooney (*Myths of the Cherokee*, pp. 292-93),
and desires to see ice in an Oklahoma Cherokee myth
(Kilpatrick and Kilpatrick, *Friends of Thunder*, pp. 9-10).
In the *i:gawé:sdi* above the bird spirit is invoked in his
compelling, soul-possessing "black" aspect.

The Cherokee terms (there are several) that we have
consistently translated as "soul," in many instances might
just as fittingly have been rendered "mind" or "heart." All
derive from the verb stem *-da:n(v)dh-* ("to think purpose-
fully").

The "White Pathways" in the ardent and beautiful
third part of this incantation symbolize the happy future
life-course of the inamorata.

◄◄◄

This charm, discovered in a Cherokee County shaman's notebook, some three-quarters of a century old, bears the simple inscription: *Age:hyv ugv:wahli* ("a woman, for the purpose of"). It is undoubtedly to be said four times, possibly adjunctive to "going to the water." A woman might use it as freely as might a man. Not a word would have to be changed: "her soul," "her name," and similar terms have no gender in Cherokee.

5.

Listen! Now You have just come to hear.
(Your name is _____; your clan is _____.)

Ha! Lonely Pathways lie before you and me.
(My body is not lonely.)

Listen! Now! Ha! My Pathway lies before me at the tree-
    tops.
Ha! I have just come to cover you with my body.

Ha! Your soul is to emerge, not the Crow!
Ha! The treetops lie before me!
He is not the victor!

Now *Age:hyv Gu:gv!*
"I have just come to turn back your soul!"
(Your clan is _____.)

Ha! Now She has just come—Ha!—to join your saliva and
    mine.
Ha! They are never to separate again!

〉〉

(Your name is _____, your people are _____; and
my name is _____, my people are _____.)

The spirit invoked but not mentioned by name until the
ninth line is one that cannot be identified with certainty
even by Cherokees. Mooney and Olbrechts (*The Swimmer Manuscript,* p. 20) are probably correct in their assumption that the term "*Age:hyv* (woman) *Gu:gv* (?)" is
an ancient ritualistic designation for the sun. Their specu-
lation that *Gu:gv* (sometimes both written and pronounced
Gu:ga) might mean "very important," or "par excellence,"
being derived from the suffix *-go:ga,* is predicated upon
less firm ground; for certainly the Cherokee shamans are
convinced that the word means "beautiful!" There is
enough resemblance between *Gu:gv* and *gu:g(u),* the term
for a bottle-shaped piece of pottery, to raise the suspicion
that both of the words derive from some ancient common
verb stem.

In affairs of the heart *uhi:soʔdi* is sometimes induced
to erase all affection of a rival and to put an individual in
a receptive state for new romantic adventures, and to
create an atmosphere of irritability and mistrust around
those individuals who are already lovers or mates. The
meaning of the third and fourth lines appears to be: "My
enchantment will hover over your future; and yet, your
future and mine are bound together. As for myself, I am
free from all enchantment: I am master of my destiny."

The figure of speech relative to a triumphal "pathway
[future]" above earthbound other men, "at the treetops,"
is a familiar one in Cherokee medicine and magic.

Many Cherokee conjurations and incantations are min-

‹‹‹

iature dramas wherein the reciter assumes several roles. "Your soul," he says to himself, "is to emerge [win out], not the Crow [the rival for the affections of the girl that he is attempting to overcome with magic]!" (The crow is often employed as the symbol of a despicable rival [cf. Mooney, "Sacred Formulas," pp. 375-79].) "I have just come to turn back your soul!" says the *Age:hyv Gv:gv* to the woman who has some degree of interest in the "Crow."

Aboriginally the Cherokees considered the saliva, not the blood, to be the vital fluid. The thirteenth and fourteenth lines echo from the forests of ancient America the statement in Genesis 2:24: ". . . and they shall be of one flesh."

This *i:gawé:sdi,* discovered at *Se:lamí:yi* in southeastern Adair County, is written upon a slip of paper that bears the date of the committal of the text to writing: April 19, 1882. Both the phraseology of the charm and the florid style of the Sequoyah symbols with which it was written speak eloquently of North Carolina, even as its septempartite form attests to its potency. Although it has no caption and no directions, it gives every indication of being the text of a "going to the water" ritual that is to be recited four times at dawn for four successive mornings.

6.

Now! I am to make my appearance!
Crow, I speak well!

Now under the Morning Red, now under the treetops I
    just submerged myself.
I, _____, have just laid down the Pathway.

My Red Attire, desired by Red Eyes, I have just come to
    spread out.

Now I have plucked them out.
They will be in my body!

You will be unable to glance away.
Your thought is not to wander.

At my back upon the Eternal White Road will be the sound
    of your footsteps.
I have just come to draw away your soul!

Now! Now You Little White Dog!
He has just come to fondle your soul.
(In what You have come to do, you are not to desist!)

(This is my name, _____; these are my people, _____.)

> "Gha?! Gha?! Gha?! Gha?!
> Di?! Di?! Di?! Di?!"

There is no equivalent in English for the Cherokee term
that means the glow of the morning sky, the *Morgenröte*,
just before the sun rises; for built into the word is the connotation that this auroral phenomenon is impregnated with
miraculous creative power. Like a disembodied spirit, says
the incantator, he has bathed in this sea of magical red
up there at the level of the treetops; he is now clothed in
radiant enchantment, and can say to a rival: "I speak with
supernatural authority!" and can say to himself: "I lay down

my own Pathway (i.e., future)!" He knows that he is the object of envious admiration, which he extracts merely to add to his already overpowering glory.

With a sudden shift in tonality this brassy rodomontade modulates into a passage that in the original language throbs with an aching ecstasy:

You will be unable to glance away.
Your thought is not to wander.

At my back upon the Eternal White Road will be the sound
    of your footsteps.
I have just come to draw away your soul!

With another surprising change of key the mood lightens and breaks into an *allegretto* with the conceit of the faithful and loving puppy romping with the affections of the woman and joyously barking.

This *i:gawé:sdi* from *Gwagwó:hi* is starkly captioned, "For the purpose of women." Since there are no lacunae in it for the insertion of the name and clan of an individual, no doubt both are stated before the series of four recitations. The *i:gawé:sdi* is probably a "going to the water" text.

7.

White Pathways are mine!
I, _____, am attired in what is mine, Black Yellow Mock-
    ingbird!

Deep in your heart, _____, You have just come to per-
    form.

>>>

Dhla:nuwa, You named me "Woman-taker!"

Dhla:nuwa, You named me "Person-taker!"

It is not uncommon for several spirits, usually those to whom similar powers are attributed, to be petitioned in the same *i:gawé:sdi.* Both the Yellow Mockingbird and the *Dhla:nuwa* are called upon here. The latter, the name of which varies somewhat from dialect to dialect (*Sa:nuwa, Dlani:gw(a)*, etc.), is not a bird spirit, but a spirit bird that existed on earth only in the mythological past. It now resides "Above." While terrestrial it was of hawklike mien, of gigantic size, and possessed man-eating proclivities. Myths concerning this fierce avian are fairly numerous (cf. Mooney, *Myths,* pp. 315-16, 466; Kilpatrick and Kilpatrick, *Friends of Thunder,* pp. 71-76). Narratives pertaining to a roclike mythic bird have been obtained from several of the tribes of the Southeast (cf. Swanton, *Myths and Tales of the Southeastern Indians,* pp. 90, 154, 193, 246-47).

In a ritualistic sense to be "attired" is to be clad in supernatural power. Here the incantator states that he is in full possession of those attributes to which his magic legitimately entitles him.

The addressing of one individual and then abruptly turning, figuratively speaking, to address another one, something which is of common occurrence in *idi:gawé:sdi,* makes for an awkwardness in the translation of the second part in the above. If we assume that the name of the girl toward whom the magic is being directed is *Wali:ya,* then the meaning of the line under consideration would be:

"Deep in your heart, *Wali:ya*, You, Black Yellow Mocking-bird, have just come to perform."

The significance of the third part is clear: "*Dhla:nuwa*, You bestowed upon me the power to capture a woman!" The meaning of the fourth part is not so self-evident, for it could be: "*Dhla:nuwa*, You bestowed upon me the power to capture a human being!" or, perhaps: "*Dhla:nuwa*, You bestowed upon me the power to capture [eliminate] a 'person' [rival]!"

A note appended to this *i:gawé:sdi* from *Tse:gí:i*, in southern Adair County, informs us that the text is to assist one in attracting a woman, and that it is to be sung. Like so much Cherokee ritualistic music, the tune is probably forever beyond recovery. We are also instructed that the charm has additional utility: it is of value "if someone scolds one"—in other words, it can patch up a lovers' quarrel. When used for the latter purpose, the lover is enjoined to go at dawn to the brink of running water, to face east, to say (not sing) the charm but once, and then to wash his face. He must do this upon four successive days.

8.

(1)

Now! In the Seventh Heaven all of You rest, You Little Men, You Great Wizards!
All of You fail in nothing.
(I have just informed all of You.)

Now You and I have just come to "remake" the Brown Tobacco.
(This is my name, _____; these are my people, _____.)

>>

Now You and I have just come to draw away the soul of a
    woman.

Then your thoughts are not to wander away!
Your soul is to be mine!
What the Brown Dog said to you, say to her!

Now you will be making a shadow behind me where I am
    walking.
"I have just come to 'remake' for you the White Tobacco!"
Now you will be standing about behind me where I am
    walking.

(2)

Now! In the Seventh Heaven all of You rest, You Little
    Men, You Great Wizards!
All of You fail in nothing.
(I have just informed all of You.)

Now You and I have just come to "remake" the Brown
    Tobacco.
(This is my name, _____; these are my people, _____.)
Now You and I have just come to draw away the soul of a
    woman.

Then your thoughts are not to wander away!
Your soul is to be mine!
What the White Dog said to you, say to her!

Now you will be making a shadow behind me where I am
    walking.

"I have just come to 'remake' for you the White Tobacco!"
Now you will be standing behind me where I am walking.

(3)

Now! In the Seventh Heaven all of You rest, You Little
Men, You Great Wizards!
All of You fail in nothing.
(I have just informed all of You.)

Now You and I have just come to "remake" the Brown
Tobacco.
(This is my name, _____; these are my people, _____.)
Now You and I have just come to draw away the soul of a
woman.

Then your thoughts are not to wander away!
Your soul is to be mine!
What the Black Dog said to you, say to her!

Now you will be making a shadow behind me where I am
walking.
"I have just come to 'remake' for you the White Tobacco!"
Now you will be standing about behind me where I am
walking.

(4)

Now! In the Seventh Heaven all of You rest, You Little
Men, You Great Wizards!
All of You fail in nothing.
(I have just informed all of You.)

‣‣‣

Now You and I have just come to "remake" the Brown
    Tobacco.
(This is my name, _____; these are my people, _____.)
Now You and I have just come to draw away the soul of a
    woman.

Then your thoughts are not to wander away!
Your soul is to be mine!
What the Blue Dog said to you, say to her!

Now you will be making a shadow behind me where I am
    walking.
"I have just come to 'remake' for you the White Tobacco!"
Now you will be standing behind me where I am walk-
    ing.

In Cherokee theology the celestial regions are conceived as being constituted of a series of seven successive
strata. The spirits that reside in those regions are thought
of as normally being in a state of blissful repose, out of
which they bestir themselves upon being properly petitioned in order to descend to earth and exercise various
powers.

One assumes that the "Little Men" importuned above
are members of the family of that Being, Thunder, whose
authority is second only to that of the Creator Himself.
As we have previously stated, the respectful reminding of
the spirit or spirits invoked of his or their infallibility is a
cliché often seen in *idi:gawé:sdi.* "I have just informed all
of You" and kindred statements are ritualisms for "I am
bringing my problem to You."

The fourth line is somewhat puzzling, for the Cherokee is quite clear: *Hv:di:na tso:la wo:dige vno:dhlvhisaʔni:ga* ("Now You [singular] and I have just come to remake the Brown Tobacco"). If "You" were in reference to the "Little Men" petitioned, the verb-form would indicate plurality in its pronominal prefix. Perhaps we deal here with a ritualistic conception wherein the combined powers of several spirits are thought of as a single force.

We hazard this as an exegesis of the ninth line: "Brown Dog" is the ceremonial designation for a divining pebble. The incantator says to himself: "You know what her future is fated to be. Tell the girl what it is." Successive statements of the *i:gawé:sdi* (all the requisite four of them are written out) gradually change the "color" of that future until the spell finally comes to rest upon the "blue" of *uhí:soʔdí*, the hue of love-longing.

"I have just come to 'remake' for you the White Tobacco!" is, of course, a spiritual voice reassuring the incantator that the tobacco, originally an earthly "Brown" in color, is going to produce happiness.

A note upon this *i:gawé:sdi* from *Tse:gí:i* reminds one that the name and clan of the girl must be stated and that *tso:lagayv́:li* should be used. This is a shaman's professional incantation for preparing tobacco for a client, and it is magic of enormous power.

9.

(1)

Now! In the Seventh Heaven all of You rest, You Little Men, You Great Wizards!

>>>

All of You fail in nothing.
He and I have just come There to inform all of You.

You must tell the Brown Dog.
Now You and I have just come to "remake" the Brown
    Tobacco.

I am _____.
Now this woman is _____.
You and I have just come to draw away her soul.

Then your thoughts are not to wander away!
I am _____!
Your soul will be mine!

(2)

Now! In the Seventh Heaven all of You rest, You Little
    Men, You Great Wizards!
All of You fail in nothing.
He and I have just come There to inform all of You.

You must tell the White Dog.
Now You and I have just come to "remake" the Brown
    Tobacco.

I am _____.
Now this woman is _____.
You and I have just come to draw away her soul.

Then your thoughts are not to wander away!
I am _____!
Your soul will be mine!

$$(3)$$

In the Seventh Heaven all of You rest, You Little Men, You
 Great Wizards!
All of You fail in nothing.
He and I have just come There to inform all of You.

You must tell the Black Dog.
Now You and I have just come to "remake" the Brown
 Tobacco.

I am _____.
Now this woman is _____.
You and I have just come to draw away her soul.

Then your thoughts are not to wander away!
I am _____!
Your soul will be mine!

$$(4)$$

Now! In the Seventh Heaven all of You rest, You Little
 Men, You Great Wizards!
All of You fail in nothing.
He and I have just come There to inform all of You.

Now Blue Dog, I am here!
Now You and I have just come to "remake" the Brown
 Tobacco.

I am _____.
Now this woman is _____.
You and I have just come to draw away her soul.

Then your thoughts are not to wander away!
I am _____!
Your soul will be mine!

In this variant of the preceding *i:gawé:sdi* we have the figure of the incantator and the divining stone rising Above together to the serene seats of the Little Men for the purpose of having those great Wizards determine the destiny of a woman.

As is often the case in Cherokee magical *idi:gawé:sdi*, one of the lines in one of the recitations is out of the pattern established (cf: "Now Blue Dog, I am here!").

Like the preceding, this incantation is from *Tse:gí:i*.

10.
These are my people: _____.

This is my name: _____.

At first glance the above would appear to be but the incipit or the termination of an *i:gawé:sdi*, yet it is complete in itself. We have seen it written in several manuscripts. It is for "remaking" in the conventional manner tobacco to be used in winning the heart of a woman who, no doubt, is named prior to the four recitations of the spell. "One goes over there where she is living and smokes a shaving of it," say the incantation's directions.

Since no spirits are invoked, one is justified in raising the question as to the source of the power with which the tobacco is infused. It comes from the name of the lover and the designation for his clan. Inasmuch as both are endowed with life and personality, both are generators of spiritual energy.

Other than relatively, one cannot say that any tobacco-"remaking" *i:gawé:sdi* is weak. In that sense this charm from *Gha:hl(i)se:ts(i) Tso:dalv*, near the mouth of Caney Creek in eastern Cherokee County, is a mild one. A layman might know it, and it could be used by a woman as well as a man.

11.

Ha! Very quickly I have just come to you, _____!

No loneliness, then!

Ha! Think of me without loneliness!

[My name is _____; my people are _____.]

The meaning of this little charm appears to be (let us assume that the girl's name is *A:li*): "I have just come in the smoke of this magic tobacco to remove your *uhí:soʔdí, A:li!* Now that I have come, it is gone forever!"

The directions accompanying the text state: "To 're-make' tobacco for a woman. If you want her to think about you, smoke in the direction in which she lives." In the absence of specific instructions, one assumes that the blowing of the smoke toward the home of the woman is to be done four times per day for four days.

This example has some features in common with the preceding one. The missing line which we have inserted could just as well be said at the beginning of the charm

>>

as at the end. There is no prescribed place for it, and as is
the case here, it is frequently omitted when a text of this
genre is written down.

This charm is from the same locale as the preceding
one. The laity might know it; a woman could use it as well
as a man.

12.

Now! Listen!
You Great Crested Flycatcher!
Quickly You have just come to hear that it was the woman.

Ha, then! You were attired like the White Tobacco.

Now! Listen!
I am as beautiful as the White Kingbird.
(Woman,—Ha!—I was attired!)

Ha! It was in the very middle of the crown of your head!
It was in the very middle of your soul!

The bird spirits referred to are those of the *Myiarchus
crinitus boreus* and the *Tyrannus tyrannus*.

The meaning of the third line would appear to be:
"Quickly You have just come to hear about what is on my
mind, an affair concerning a woman."

Commonly the supernatural qualities in which an individual is "attired" are understood to be identical with
those attributed to a specific spirit. In the fourth line above
the reciter of this *i:gawé:sdi* addresses himself reassuringly
to the effect that he has become invested with the powers

of "remade" tobacco, which is sometimes alluded to even conversationally as "white tobacco (*tso:lune:gv*)."

It would seem that in the last two lines the incantator is exultantly announcing to the woman where the force of the "remade" tobacco is to strike her; for although this spell has no caption, unquestionably it is for preparing tobacco. Magic hitting in "the very middle of the crown" of her head will addle her thought; striking her in the heart (the soul is conceived to be in the heart), it will shatter her will to resist the charms of her enchanter.

In the crumbling remains of what had been a huge black gum tree upon the left bank of Tenkiller Lake, in Cherokee County, there was discovered in the spring of 1964 a sealed glass fruit jar. Apparently it had been secreted in a hollow of the black gum while the tree was still standing. The container was full of moldering manuscripts written in Sequoyah syllabary. Upon one of the sodden and faded papers in the jar was inscribed this magical gem.

13.
You White Great Crested Flycatcher!

Your Place of Peace is Above.

Very quickly You have just come.

Ha! You have just come to remake the White Tobacco!

Ha! You White Kingbird!

Ha! Very quickly You have just come.

Ha! You have just come to remake the White Tobacco!

Although this incantation from *Gha:hl(i)se:ts(i) Tso:-dalv* is but a variant of the preceding *i:gawé:sdi*, it possesses a significant attribute of its own. For all of its smallish size and rather commonplace wording, it is a siege gun for the reducing of one of the more formidable of the citadels of Eros; for it is in true seven-part format. It is forthrightly labeled: "To 'remake' tobacco for women."

The shaman who wrote it down affixed to it a reminder to himself that a name must be stated after each of the four deliveries of the spell. Now inasmuch as the *i:gawé:sdi* is a text employed by a medicine man to prepare tobacco for a client, one may well wonder whose name is stated—that of the medicine man, or that of the lover who is going to use the tobacco. The name of the lover would be used. The client would be present when the tobacco-"remaking" ritual was enacted. After each time that the shaman murmured the above words (the client would be fortunate to catch a single one of them), the lover would first speak his name, after which he would bestow a little explosive expectoration upon the tobacco and then blow his breath upon it.

14.

Now! Listen! Now, *Dhla:nuwa!*
Ha! You are a Great Wizard.
You fail in nothing.

Ha! You have just come to elevate the White Tobacco.
(Her name is _____; her people are _____.)

<<<<<<<<<<<<<<<<<<<<<<<<<<<<<<<<<<<<<<<<<<<<<<<<<

You and I have just come to elevate her soul!

Listen! Raven!
You are a Great Wizard!
You fail in nothing.

Ha! You have just come to bring the White Tobacco.
(Her name is _____; her people are _____.)
You have just come to bring her soul!

One observes that each of the two spirits mentioned in
this tobacco-remaking *i:gawé:sdi* performs a definite task
that is consistent in each case with the character attributed to him. The huge, fierce, and high-flying *Dhla:nuwa*
whisks the soul of the woman and the addling smoke of
the magic tobacco together to dizzy heights of bewilder-
ment. The stealthy black Raven (*Corvus corax principalis?*)
surreptitiously carries the enchanted fumes to the unsuspecting victim, and then comes triumphantly winging
back with her overpowered soul. She is first shaken and
dazzled, then subtly overcome.

This imaginative *i:gawé:sdi* was penned with a callig-
raphy almost microscopic in size in a thick but tiny notebook found in the effects of a deceased medicine man of
Dhlv:datsí:i in southwestern Adair County. The directions
appended to it merely state that it is for "remaking" tobacco "for women," and that it is to be said four times—
both facts which are patent.

15.

Now! Listen!

You reside Above, Red Hawk!

>>

You Two have just come to halt in the very middle of your
   soul.

(This is your name, _____.)

Your soul is mine!

It is not to wander off.

Your soul is mine alone!

The word for the Red ("triumphal"-colored) Hawk is
the generic term employed for accipitres. The use of such
a word is something quite out of the ordinary: as a rule a
bird spirit is pinpointed with specificity.

The "You Two" in the third line are almost certainly
those handsome midgets, the Sons of Thunder (cf. Mooney
and Olbrechts, *The Swimmer Manuscript*, pp. 23-24);
"your soul," of course, is in reference to the soul of the
girl against whom the incantator is "working."

This *i:gawé:sdi* was seen in a very small pocket notebook that apparently had once been the possession of a
long-dead medicine man from *Diga:da:yo:sdí:i*, in northern
Sequoyah County. "To 'remake' tobacco for a woman" is
the footnote to the incantation.

16.

Like the Red Lightning . . .

Like the Fog . . .

Like the Panther . . .

Like the Red Wolf . . .

Like You, You Wizard, I have just come to make my appearance.

I will be walking in the very middle of your soul.

Now! Now the Smoke of the White Tobacco has just come to wing down upon you!

After one has pointed out what is gloriously obvious—that the above is the work of a lyric genius—there is little that one can say. Even in the naked light of an alien tongue this exquisitely polished gem gleams; in the soft shadows of its ancient Iroquoian setting it is indeed incandescent:

Anagali:sgi gigagé:i iyú:sdi . . .
U:ghvhada iyú:sdi . . .
Dhlv:datsi iyú:sdi . . .
Wahhya gigagé:i iyú:sdi . . .
Hida:we:h(i) iyú:sdi tsinanugó:tsi:gá.
Tsada:n(v)dho:gi ayv aye:hliyu gai:se:sdi.
Gha?! Hna:gwo tso:la uné:gv tsugh(a)sv́:sdi tsa:yalv́:tsi:gá
    tsugh(a)sv́:sdi!

The identity of the "Wizard" mentioned in the fifth line is never established.

The fashioner of this verbal jewel perhaps lived (and, one may suspect, deeply loved) before Jacob saw Rachel at the well on the Plain of Aram. His dream lives on in a tattered notebook found in a trunk of papers in a cabin on Hummingbird Branch, near Echota Church in western Adair County. Its deceased recorder had been a resident of *Gha:hl(i)se:ts(i) Tso:dalv.*

"For women. One uses tobacco," is the laconic comment upon sheer beauty.

17.

Now! Listen!
You and I are truly set apart!

It was Decided that you think of me.
You think of my entire body.
You think of me from your very soul.
You think of me, never to forget that I walk about.

This is my name, ————.
I am a man!

The mourning doves will be calling: *"Gu:le! Hu:! Hu:! Hu:! Hu:!"*
You say, you woman, that your name is ————, that your people are ————.

No spirit-helper is called upon here; in fact, both format and flavor of this idyllic *i:gawé:sdi* are quite unusual.

That gentle bird, the mourning dove (*Zeaidura macroura carolinensis*), bears for Cherokee society almost identically the same poetic significance it has for Europeans. To Cherokees it is a symbol of young love, of conjugal fidelity and bliss, and they, like the white man, hear in its cry a subdued grief. Their word for acorn(s) is *gu:le;* to their ears that is what the dove says in its calling. Their word for the bird, *gu:le disgo:hnihi,* means "crier for acorns."

The above text presents no internal evidence that it is

for "remaking" tobacco, but a footnote states that such is its purpose. It is written in a large ledger book from *Gwagwó:hi,* most of which is devoted to the recording of Oklahoma Cherokee myths.

18.

Now! Leave your soul in my body, _____!
Leave your speech in my body, _____!
Leave your blood in my body, _____!
Leave it, _____!

My people are _____: (your soul and mine are one!).
My people are _____: (your song and mine are one!).
My people are _____: (your attire and mine are one!).
My people are _____: (your saliva and mine are one!).

Now! This is your name: _____.

Mourning Dove, I have just requested You to go get me a servant.
(In the very middle of the crown of my head You have just come to alight!)

Mourning Dove, I have just requested You to go get me a servant.
(In the very middle of my forehead You have just come to alight!)

Mourning Dove, I have just requested You to go get me a servant.
(In the very middle of my breast You have just come to alight!)

Mourning Dove, I have just requested You to go get me a
   servant.
   (In the very middle of my soul You have just come to
   alight!)

Now! Red *Dhla:nuwa*, very quickly You have just come
   down to prepare it!

   This highly unconventional tobacco-"remaking" *i:ga-
wé:sdi*, seen in the same ledger from which the preceding
example came, contains few obscurities. By "servant" is
meant "wife," of course; and what the *Dhla:nuwa* has come
"to prepare" is the tobacco over which the incantation is
being said.
   The caption informs that this *i:gawé:sdi*, to be said four
times, is for making "medicine" for a woman.

19.

Now! Listen! You Great Wizard!
"I have just come to put the saliva of the Cat Himself into
   your mouth!"

Ha, then! You Great Wizard!
"Ha, then! Over there I have just come to put the saliva of
   the very Spider Himself into your mouth!"

(This is your name: _____.)

Ha, then! I have just come to envelop you in the saliva of
   the Spider so that your soul will not divide!

Ha, then! There is no loneliness!
The Pathway closes at the White House!

The Ancient One now has just come to make the Fire rise
to its feet!

(This is your name and mine: _____, _____.)

Mooney (*Myths*, p. 546) is of the opinion that *we:sa*,
the Cherokee term for cat, is a loan-word from English, an
attempt to say "pussy." This incantation lends no comfort
to such a supposition; for here the term is nestled among
archaic word-forms of such formidability as to separate
swiftly those who are Cherokees from those who study the
Cherokees. Certainly the "Cat" here is not the house cat
that was introduced from Europe. We suspect that the
word may be the designation for some extinct animal once
known to the Cherokees, not necessarily a feline. The term
may have been revived and applied to the white man's
domestic companion.

An individual whose principal body secretion, his saliva,
has been replaced by the saliva of spirits has acquired the
powers of those supernatural beings. The incantator does
not state here to what use he puts his Cat-power; but what
he does with his Spider-power he announces in a line of
very great beauty, the meaning of which is: "I have just
come to enchant you, so that your love will be for me
alone."

With another glowing line he states: "The Pathway
closes at the White House (Your fate is to be happiness
in my home)!" Then mounting to even greater poetic alti-

tude he proclaims: "The Ancient One has just come to
make the Fire rise to its feet! (The Provider Himself has
just come to infuse this tobacco, when it is set alight, with
His Spirit)."

Literary reputations have been founded on less than
this superb poem made in the wild free dawn of American
man.

A notation upon this *i:gawé:sdi* from *Gha:hl(i)se:ts(i)
Tso:dalv* says: "To prepare tobacco for women. Early in
the morning. Four times."

20.

The White Tobacco has just descended to you and me from
    Above.

The Wizard fails in nothing!

The White Pipe has just descended to you and me from
    Above.

The Wizard fails in nothing: you and I are never to part!

One cannot be absolutely certain who the "Wizard" is
that "remakes" the tobacco which, when smoked in the
"White Pipe," will bring lifelong conjugal contentment.
Spirits are no less willing and able to perform if not addressed by name.

This neatly turned little *i:gawé:sdi* is an incantation
that any layman could use if he could obtain possession
of it. Its straightforwardness, reflected in its format and

wording, would offer no problems. English translations give few hints of the frustrating difficulties in both memorization and pronunciation that some of the medicine man's professional *idi:gawé:sdi* present. They abound in tricky quasi-repetitions, and the language used is sometimes as far removed from contemporary Cherokee dialects as is Chaucer from Joyce.

"To 'remake' tobacco for women" is the caption upon this *Gha:hl(i)se:ts(i) Tso:dalv* incantation.

21.

The Yellow Spider fails in nothing, _____, you woman!
Now He and I have just come to draw away your soul.
My soul, _____'s, They have just come to put in the
    Seven Clan Districts.
Ancient Tobacco!
Now You have just come to assist me!
I am to fail in nothing!
I am a Little Man!

The Red Spider fails in nothing, _____, you woman!
Now He and I have just come to draw away your soul.
My soul, _____'s, They have just come to put in the
    Seven Clan Districts.
Ancient Tobacco!
Now You have just come to assist me!
I am to fail in nothing!
I am a Little Man!

The Blue Spider fails in nothing, _____, you woman!
Now He and I have just come to draw away your soul.

My soul, _____'s, They have just come to put in the
   Seven Clan Districts.
Ancient Tobacco!
Now You have just come to assist me!
I am to fail in nothing!
I am a Little Man!

The Black Spider fails in nothing, _____, you woman!
Now He and I have just come to draw away your soul.
My soul, _____'s, They have just come to put in the
   Seven Clan Districts.
Ancient Tobacco!
Now You have just come to assist me!
I am to fail in nothing!
I am a Little Man!

The Spider, a creature of cunning and stealth, is fairly
frequently enlisted in the service of the Cherokee lovesick,
Eastern and Western (cf. Mooney, "Sacred Formulas," pp.
382-83). There can be no doubt that in the above *i:gawé:-
sdi* the Spider is assigned a color in accordance with the
direction from which he arrives to help the lover capture
the soul of the girl named. The Spider arrives, as one sees,
from all directions; His influence is everywhere. The cor-
respondence between the various colors and the cardinal
compass points is this: Yellow—south; Red—east; Blue—
north; Black—west. One notes that the arrivals are in a se-
quence resulting from counterclockwise progression around
the compass—which is the "good," or the "right," manner
of circling.
   The meaning of the third line is probably this: "They

[the Spider and the Ancient Tobacco] have just come to make me attractive wherever I go."

Cherokees hold Thunder to be their especial friend and protector (Kilpatrick and Kilpatrick, *Friends of Thunder*, pp. 50-51). His relatives are those kindly, helpful, exceedingly mighty Little People (cf. *Friends of Thunder*, pp. 77-95; Witthoft and Hadlock, "Cherokee-Iroquois Little People," *Journal of American Folklore*, LIX, 413-22, *passim*). The one who delivers the above incantation assures himself to the effect that as a result of the supernatural aid of the Spider and the *tso:lagayv:li* he has become invested with the abilities and qualities of one of these spirit midgets.

The caption upon this Cherokee County shaman's incantation is routinely informative: "To 'remake' tobacco for a woman. Four times. Early in the morning."

22.

Now! Listen!
I am as beautiful as the *Tsugv:tsala:la!*
I am as beautiful as the Redheaded Woodpecker!
I am as beautiful as the Bluebird!

All of You have just come to purchase the Red.

Ha! Red *Dhla:nuwa!*
(The Smoke of the Tobacco has just come to purchase you!)

Ha, then! This Blue Smoke has just come to pierce holes in the very middle of her soul itself.

It is to fail in nothing.

Now! Now one assumes that the Blue Smoke has just come
    to pierce holes.

Ha, then! You purchased her soul!

(This is your name, you woman: _____; and these are
    your people: _____.)

   While the term *tsugv:tsala:la,* according to Witthoft
("Bird Lore of the Eastern Cherokees," *Journal of the
Washington Academy of Sciences,* XXXVI, pp. 382-83),
is applied by the Eastern Cherokees to the black-and-
white warbler (*Mniotilta varia*), and while to our knowledge it is sometimes applied in Oklahoma to at least one
and perhaps several species of orioles (*Icterus*), the real
Tsugv:tsala:la is a spirit bird, radiantly beautiful, in appearance nearest to a quail (Kilpatrick and Kilpatrick,
Friends of Thunder, pp. 94-95). He is kindly disposed
toward lovers.
   The woodpecker is, of course, the *Melanerpes erythro-
cephalus,* the bluebird the *Sialia sialis sialis.*
   The precise meaning of the statement, "All of You have
just come to purchase the Red," is not readily perceived;
however, since red is the color of success, it would seem
that the thought at the heart of the statement is this: "All
of You Bird Wizards have just come with your powers for
the purpose of ensuring success." Later in the incantation
we find the Smoke of the "remade" Tobacco coming to purchase, and then later purchasing, the soul of the girl desig-

nated by name. Any use in Cherokee magic or medicine of a verb-form derived from the stem *-hwa:-* ("to purchase") is eye-catching because of its rarity.

This is another *i:gawé:sdi* that was recovered from the glass jar mentioned in No. 12. Its caption states: "To 'remake' tobacco for a woman. Tobacco 'medicine' for smoking."

23.

(1)

Now! Listen! White Bluebird!
Quickly You have just come to hear.
You are a Great Wizard.

Ha! Now quickly You Great Wizard and I have just come
    to poultice with the White Tobacco!
(This is her name: _____; these are her people: _____.)
Ha! Now! Now You and I have just come to draw out her
    soul with the Smoke of the White Tobacco!

Now my soul has just come over there to go under her soul,
    which will be unable to think of others!

Now, one assumes, unknowingly it has just come to go
    under it!

(2)

Now! Listen! White *Tsugv:tsala:la!*
Quickly You have just come to hear.
You are a Great Wizard.

Ha! Now quickly You Great Wizard and I have just come
    to poultice with the White Tobacco!
(This is her name: _____; these are her people: _____.)
Ha! Now! Now You and I have just come to draw out her
    soul with the Smoke of the White Tobacco!

Now my soul has just come over there to go under her soul,
    which will be unable to think of others!

Now, one assumes, unknowingly it has just come to go
    under it!

(3)

Now! Listen! Red *Di:sdi!*
Quickly You have just come to hear.
You are a Great Wizard.

Ha! Now quickly You Great Wizard and I have just come
    to poultice with the White Tobacco!
(This is her name: _____; these are her people: _____.)
Ha! Now! Now You and I have just come to draw out her
    soul with the Smoke of the White Tobacco!

Now my soul has just come over there to go under her soul,
    which will be unable to think of others!

Now, one assumes, unknowingly it has just come to go
    under it!

(4)

Now! Listen! Red Purple Martin!

Quickly You have just come to hear.
You are a Great Wizard.

Ha! Now quickly You Great Wizard and I have just come
   to poultice with the White Tobacco!
(This is her name: _____; these are her people: _____.)
Ha! Now! Now You and I have just come to draw out her
   soul with the Smoke of the White Tobacco!

Now my soul has just come over there to go under her soul,
   which will be unable to think of others!

Now, one assumes, unknowingly it has just come to go
   under it!

   The panel of spirit birds and bird spirits appealed to
here are, in Cherokee thought, one and all of high usefulness in affairs amorous. The *Di:sdi* is a spirit bird, generally
thought of as being small and blue. Like the *Tsugv:tsala:la*,
it may be the lingering remembrance of an extinct avian,
or one that was once known to the Cherokees when they
were living somewhere other than in their historic seats,
perhaps millennia ago. The martin, which the Cherokees
call a *dhlu:dhlu* (an imitation of its call), is the *Progne
subis subis*.
   We can offer no ready explanation why two of the avian
Wizards are clothed in the "white" of peace, happiness,
attainment, and the other two in the "red" of power and
success.
   The figurative poulticing with magical tobacco in order
to draw out the soul of the woman has a parallel in Chero-

kee therapy whereby a tobacco poultice, likewise endued
with supernatural qualities, is employed for the purpose of
extracting pains and small foreign objects "shot" into the
body of a victim by an evil "thinker."

The conceit of one soul tunneling under, or burrowing
under, the stronghold of another one is frequently seen.
One wonders if it does not derive from an aboriginal mili-
tary tactic. The basic concept is central in a charming un-
reported myth concerning a mole who burrows under a
storehouse in order to steal tobacco for a human friend.

This *i:gawé:sdi* from *Gha:hl(i)se:ts(i) Tso:dalv* is, pat-
ently, a professional one. "To 'remake' tobacco for women"
is its caption.

24.

Now! Listen!
Your Place of Peace is Above, You Little Man.
You are a Wizard.

You have just come to change my course.

Now You will be searching for a sweetheart.

"Sayi:! Dami:!"

In Cherokee magic *"Sayi:!"* and *"Dami:!"* are onomato-
poeic for a flash of lightning, and also for a movement of
dazzling speed. In the above they symbolize the haste with
which the Thunderer sets out to accomplish the mission
desired of him—to find for the incantator a girl friend.

"To 'remake' tobacco. To put into the hand and to
blow," says the footnote to this *i:gawé:sdi* from *Tse:gí:i.*

II
CREATING LONELINESS

II

CREATING LONELINESS

1.

Now! The Whippoorwill knows that I just struck you,
_____, you woman!

I just turned over your soul.

Sleepless, you will be unable to think of anything else!

[My name is _____; my people are _____.]

Uhí:so?dí-producing incantations create effects leading
to unpredictable results; therefore, they have a folk-repu-
tation inclining to the sinister. Perhaps it is fitting that the
spirit of the whippoorwill, a bird in rather poor repute
among the Cherokees, should be invoked in an *i:gawé:sdi*
such as this one.

"To turn one's soul" or "to turn over one's soul" in
Cherokee equates with "to cause one's mind to be con-
fused, or distraught" in English.

There can be little doubt but that the above incantation
is fairly dark-hued love-magic, such as one might direct
toward a woman with pre-existing commitments. It has no
caption and no directions. Seemingly it is to be said four
times, with the addition of some such line as we have
supplied.

>>>

It is from *Dhlv:datsí:i,* a few miles southwest of Stilwell, in Adair County.

2.

Now! Wild Goose!
It has been witnessed Above that You and I will become
    Great Wizards.

Ha, now! Loneliness will be found for her!
(This is the name of the woman: _____, and these are
    her people: _____.)

Already You and I have just come to keep her Image.

Now! You White Sea Gull!
As one let us be clutching hold of her forever!

   Mooney and Olbrechts (*The Swimmer Manuscript,* p.
249) state that the word for wild goose that is used in the
above, *daga:hl(a)ga,* is specifically in reference to the
American white-fronted goose (*Anser albifrons gambeli*).
Such may have been the case in North Carolina in the
period of the investigations of these ethnographers; the
Oklahoma Cherokees apparently use the term more in the
sense of a generic designation for all wild geese. Similarly
the term *u:hli* is applied to any sort of sea gull.
   The line, "Already You and I have just come to keep
her Image," may mean, "Already You and I have just come
to imprison her soul," but we cannot be certain of it.
   This is another incantation with built-in literary quality.
It was written in a very small pocket notebook by the son

of a redoubtable Natchez-Cherokee medicine man from the Natchez enclave which is partially in Sequoyah County and partially in Muskogee County. The evidence points toward the son's having recorded here an item from his late father's repertoire.

It is captioned: "To make a woman lonely."

3.

Now! Your Place of Peace is Above, White Spider!

You have just come down from Above.
(My clan is named _____.)

He has just come to envelop her soul in His tracery.
He has performed where the Peoples of the Seven Clans
   have just come to make a Shadow.

Loneliness has just caught up with them.
Eyes have just come to alight.
One of the Eyes has just alighted.

Where can her soul come forth?
Throughout the Night He did not say.
The Important One was performing, unable to be traced!

The White Spider will lead you captive!
(The soul of the woman is not to free itself!)

Now, one assumes! Now, one assumes!

The opulent imagery of this *uhí:soʔdí*-engendering in-

>>

cantation is itself akin to witchcraft. If one allows for the
unavoidable infelicities of the translation, what stands forth
is unalloyed poetry.

Often encountered in Cherokee medicine, but seldom
to be found in Cherokee magic, the term "Important One"
is a circumlocution for a mysterious and minatory force.
In this instance it is, of course, the Spider, who secretly
weaves a web in the shadow of mankind in order to trap
the soul of a woman.

This striking *i:gawé:sdi* was written upon a loose sheet
of paper that formed part of a collection of medico-magical
writings made by a traditionalist who once lived a few
miles north of *Gwagwó:hi,* in Cherokee County.

Since there is no place in this incantation, apparently
one that is merely to be said the usual four times, for either
the name or clan of the girl that the incantator seeks to
attract, presumably both name and clan are stated before
beginning the recitations. The caption is merely: "For a
woman."

4.

(1)

Wa-hi! Wa-hi! Wa-hi! Wa-hi!

I, I am a Wizard.
I just took your heart away from you.
Already I have just taken it away from you.

I, I am a Wizard.
I just took your heart away from you.
Throughout the night your soul will be lonely.

Already I have taken it away from you.

I, I am a Wizard.
Your heart was just taken by me.
Throughout the night your soul will be lonely.

Your heart, I, I am a Wizard.

Wa-hi! Wa-hi! Wa-hi! Wa-hi! Wa-hi!

Your heart! Your heart!
Dhla:nuwa!
"Gigi! Gigi!"
He just took your heart away from you.
Already He has taken it away from you.

The *Dhla:nuwa* just carried it away.
He just took your heart away from you.
Throughout the night your soul will be lonely.
Already He has taken it away from you.

The *Dhla:nuwa* just took it away from you.
"Gigi! Gigi!"
He just took your heart away from you.

The Eagle just took it away from you.
Throughout the night your soul will be lonely.
Already He has taken it away from you.
He just took your heart away from you.
The Eagle just took it away from you.

(2)
Wa-hi! Wa-hi! Wa-hi! Wa-hi! Wa-hi!

I, I am a Wizard.
I just took your heart away from you.
Already I have just taken it away from you.

I, I am a Wizard.
I just took your heart away from you.
Throughout the night your soul will be lonely.
Already I have just taken it away from you.

I, I am a Wizard.
Your heart was just taken by me.
Throughout the night your soul will be lonely.

Your heart, I, I am a Wizard.

Wa-hi! Wa-hi! Wa-hi! Wa-hi! Wa-hi!

Your heart! Your heart!
Dhla:nuwa!
"Gigi! Gigi!"
He just took your heart away from you.
Already He has taken it away from you.

The *Dhla:nuwa* just carried it away.
He just took your heart away from you.
Throughout the night your soul will be lonely.
Already He has taken it away from you.

The *Dhla:nuwa* just took it away from you.
"Gigi! Gigi!"
He just took your heart away from you.

The Long-eared Owl just took it away from you.
Throughout the night your soul will be lonely.
Already He has taken it away from you.
He just took your heart away from you.
The Long-eared Owl just took it away from you.

(3)

Wa-hi! Wa-hi! Wa-hi! Wa-hi! Wa-hi!

I, I am a Wizard.
I just took your heart away from you.
Already I have just taken it away from you.

I, I am a Wizard.
I just took your heart away from you.
Throughout the night your soul will be lonely.
Already I have taken it away from you.

I, I am a Wizard.
Your heart was just taken by me.
Throughout the night your soul will be lonely.

Your heart, I, I am a Wizard.

Wa-hi! Wa-hi! Wa-hi! Wa-hi! Wa-hi!

Your heart! Your heart!

Dhla:nuwa!
"*Gigi! Gigi!*"
He just took your heart away from you.
Already He has taken it away from you.

The *Dhla:nuwa* just carried it away.
He just took your heart away from you.
Throughout the night your soul will be lonely.
Already He has taken it away from you.

The *Dhla:nuwa* just took it away from you.
"*Gigi! Gigi!*"
He just took your heart away from you.

The Dog just took it away from you.
Throughout the night your soul will be lonely.
Already He has taken it away from you.
He just took your heart away from you.
The Dog just took it away from you.

(4)
Wa-hi! Wa-hi! Wa-hi! Wa-hi! Wa-hi!

I, I am a Wizard.
I just took your heart away from you.
Already I have just taken it away from you.

I, I am a Wizard.
I just took your heart away from you.
Throughout the night your soul will be lonely.
Already I have taken it away from you.

I, I am a Wizard.
Your heart was just taken by me.
Throughout the night your soul will be lonely.

Your heart, I, I am a Wizard.

Wa-hi! Wa-hi! Wa-hi! Wa-hi! Wa-hi!

Your heart! Your heart!
Dhla:nuwa!
"Gigi! Gigi!"
He just took your heart away from you.
Already He has taken it away from you.

The *Dhla:nuwa* just carried it away.
He just took your heart away from you.
Throughout the night your soul will be lonely.
Already He has taken it away from you.

The *Dhla:nuwa* just took it away from you.
"Gigi! Gigi!"
He just took your heart away from you.

The Barred Owl just took it away from you.
Throughout the night your soul will be lonely.
Already He has taken it away from you.
He just took your heart away from you.
The Barred Owl just took it away from you.

The Cherokee language has an utterly fantastic number

>>>

of forms for each verb—possibly something like one hundred thousand. Here in this uncharacteristically lengthy *i:gawé:sdi* various of the forms of the verb *-ig:-* ("to take") are juxtaposed in fanciful, rondeau-like patterns.

The repetitions of *"Wa-hi!"*—apparently meaningless syllables that no doubt are to be sung, not spoken—are puzzling; for they come in sets of five, not the ritualistically standard four.

"Gigi! Gigi!" is the cry of the *Dhla:nuwa* in response to the calling of his name.

The presence of the Dog among birds of prey is quite unexpected. One is entitled to be suspicious of a copyist's error. If error there be, instead of *gi:hli* ("dog"), the correct word perhaps should be *gi:ya*, an abbreviation for *gi:yági:yá*, the term for sparrow hawk (see Part III, No. 9). In the Sequoyah syllabary the whole question hinges upon the substitution of but a single symbol for another.

According to Mooney (*Myths*, p. 281), the eagle of the historic seats of the Cherokees was the golden, or war, eagle (*Aquila chrysoetus*). It was greatly reverenced. There is an Oklahoma myth (Kilpatrick and Kilpatrick, *Friends of Thunder*, pp. 135-37) wherein Thunder deputizes the Eagle to rule the earth.

Both the long-eared owl (*Asio wilsonianus*) and the barred owl (*Strix varia*), but especially the former, have sinister reputations among the Cherokees. Sorcerers frequently assume the forms of these birds.

This *i:gawé:sdi*, for "remaking" *uhí:soʔdí*-causing tobacco, is from the same source as No. 3. Its caption: "If one wants to prepare tobacco. This which is written is for a woman."

5.

(1)

Now! I am attired as Redly as is the *Dhla:nuwa!*
I have triumphed over the Clan Districts.
I have just come to pass through your soul.

Now! Now White Smoke!
With the smoke of the Red White Smoke I have just come
    to draw away your soul.
In the White Smoke now my body has just come to settle
    upon your soul.
My body has just come to wing down upon it.

Now! As filled with life as the Clan Districts, never to
    remove its gaze until it vanishes, loneliness has just
    become your fate.

Now! The Black *Dhla:nuwa* has just come to cling to you!

(2)

Now! I am attired as Redly as is the *Dhla:nuwa.*
I have triumphed over the Clan Districts.
I have just come to pass through your soul.

Now! Now White Smoke!
With the smoke of the Red White Smoke I have just come
    to draw away your soul.
In the White Smoke now my body has just come to settle
    upon your soul.
My body has just come to wing down upon it.

Now! As filled with life as the Clan Districts, never to
remove its gaze until it vanishes, loneliness has just
become your fate.

Now! The Black Eagle has just come to cling to you!

(3)

Now! I am attired as Redly as is the *Dhla:nuwa*.
I have triumphed over the Clan Districts.
I have just come to pass through your soul.

Now! Now White Smoke!
With the smoke of the Red White Smoke I have just come
to draw away your soul.
In the White Smoke now my body has just come to settle
upon your soul.
My body has just come to wing down upon it.

Now! As filled with life as the Clan Districts, never to
remove its gaze until it vanishes, loneliness has just
become your fate.

Now! The Black Long-eared Owl has just come to cling
to you!

(4)

Now! I am attired as Redly as is the *Dhla:nuwa*.
I have triumphed over the Clan Districts.
I have just come to pass through your soul.

Now! Now White Smoke!

With the smoke of the Red White Smoke I have just come
    to draw away your soul.
In the White Smoke now my body has just come to settle
    upon your soul.
My body has just come to wing down upon it.

Now! As filled with life as the Clan Districts, never to
    remove its gaze until it vanishes, loneliness has just
    become your fate.

Now! The Black Raven has just come to cling to you!

Throughout the ages poets have won the hearts of their
ladies with words that not only did not possess the pre-
tentions to magical qualities that these possess, but which
were also intrinsically far less beautiful. To point out a
single detail, surely this line is indeed radiant with magic:

"Now! As filled with life as the Clan Districts, never to
    remove its gaze until it vanishes, loneliness has just
    become your fate."

The caption upon this exquisite *uhi:soʔdí*-projector
from *Gwagwó:hi* tells us that it is for remaking tobacco
"for women," and that the tobacco should be smoked
"nearby [i.e., the smoke should be blown upon the woman
that is desired]."

6.

Now! Now, my Provider, I have just come to inform You.

>>

Very quickly You and I have just distributed about our
    Restingplace the Smoke of the White Tobacco.

The Seven Clans are not to climb over You and me.
You and I have just come to go under one of the Clans,
    so that her soul will not think of others.

Now early in the morning the Mourning Dove has just
    come to hear.
The Blue Sea Gull has just come to hear.

The Blue Smoke from the bright Sun has just come to
    cover you.
Loneliness has just come to strike you.

The Yellow Raven has just come to hear.
The Black Loneliness of Night has just come to cover you.

(Your name is _____; your people are _____.)

While the manuscript medico-religious literature indis-
putably proves the contention of Mooney and Olbrechts
(*The Swimmer Manuscript,* p. 20) that the aboriginal
Cherokees believed in a Supreme Being, it offers little in
support of their equation of this Force with the sun. Their
translation of *une:hlanv:hi,* the most commonly employed
designation for the Supreme Being as "He has apportioned,
allotted, divided into equal parts," which, say they, is in
reference to the "time-dividing role of the sun," is, like
many another of their translations, faulty. The term comes
from the verb "to provide." While upon other occasions

we have followed the precedent of Mooney and Olbrechts in their use of "Apportioner," this would appear to be as good a time as any for correcting an error that has existed far too long—hence "Provider," as seen above.

"The Seven Clans are not to climb over You and Me" contains a form of the verb *-wo:hilad-* (alternately *-wo:-iladh-*) which means to go over, by use of the feet, some sort of fence or stockade. Some expression of this concept, no doubt derived from ancient warfare against palisaded settlements, is not infrequently seen in medico-religious manuscripts.

One would assume that the line, "You and I have just come to go under one of the Clans, so that her soul will not think of others," is in allusion to the thwarting of the aspirations of, or perhaps to the nullification of the magic of, a rival from some clan other than that of the incantator. There exists manuscript data evidencing that formerly certain of the clans, and perhaps all of them, possessed magical knowledge peculiar to each.

The instructions accompanying this *Gi:dhahyó:hi* incantation for making a woman "lonely" are exceptionally detailed: While kneading tobacco held in the left hand, one begins to recite the *i:gawé:sdi* upon leaving one's home at dawn in order to "go to the water." It is to be said three times en route. Upon arriving at the water one faces east and washes one's face. One gathers a small heap of drift debris, such as leaves and twigs, and burns it. Ashes from its burning are rubbed upon the forehead and chest. A coal from this fire is used to light the tobacco, which one has put into a pipe. This one smokes while walking home. Upon the way four puffs of smoke are blown in the direc-

tion where the desired girl lives, or at that time happens
to be. After having started home, one must not turn back.
Upon arriving home, one knocks out the ashes from the
pipe in the "middle of the house."

7.
(1)

Now! Red Wild Goose!
You originated Above.
You are a Great Wizard.
You fail in nothing.

Ha! You and I have just come to "remake" the Black To-
    bacco.
Quickly it already has just come to intoxicate the soul of
    the woman.

The Blue Tobacco Moth has just come to trouble her soul.
In the middle of it He has just come to drink her blood.
(The people of the woman are _____.)

Ha! The Blue Pathways of her and of loneliness will be
    converging.
Loneliness and the Little Blue Woman will be traveling
    enclosed together.
In sleepless loneliness she will be thinking—Ha!—of me
    alone.

(2)

Red Yellow Mockingbird!
You originated Above.

You are a Great Wizard.
You fail in nothing.

Now! You and I have just come to "remake" the Black
    Tobacco.
Quickly You and I have just come to plant in her a post.
(He has just come to intoxicate the soul of the woman!)

The Blue Tobacco Moth has just come to trouble her soul.
In the middle of it He has come to drink her blood.
(The people of the woman are _____.)

Now! The Blue Pathways of her and of loneliness will be
    converging.
Loneliness and the Little Blue Woman will be traveling
    enclosed together.
In sleepless loneliness she will be thinking.

As is the case in many another *i:gawé:sdi,* the two sections of this one are quite similar but not identical. The
difficulty in memorizing treacherous near-repetitions such
as the above no doubt contributed greatly to the medicine men's writing down of their lore, and thus to its
preservation. The entire incantation above is, of course, to
be said a total of four times.

The ancient Cherokees went to school to Nature with
a spirit that can best be defined as scientific. Their poetry
reflects the intensity with which they observed natural
phenomena. The figure of the Tobacco Moth is a case
in point: the connection between the seemingly aimless
fluttering in the dusk of the nervous Tobacco Moth and

the distraught state of the woman, tormented by lovesickness, is a logical one.

This shaman's *uhí:soʔdí*-confector, labeled "To 'remake'
tobacco for a woman," is an item in the collection found
near Echota (see Part I, No. 16).

III

"REBEAUTIFYING" AND "REMAKING"

III

"REBEAUTIFYING" AND "REMAKING"

1.

Now! White Pathways will be lying before me!

Now! These are my people: _____; this is my name: _____.

Now I will not be standing about in loneliness.

Now! Very quickly I gather spiritual wisdom: I am surpassingly beautiful!

The thought in the last two lines is this: "The erotic magic of no rival is going to have any power over me because I have already been made supernaturally attractive to the opposite sex."

Seemingly a person of either sex might use this *ado:-du:hiso?dí:yi* charm from *Gwagwó:hi*. Neither caption nor directions accompany it, but inasmuch as *idi:gawé:sdi* of its genre customarily have an adjunctive ritual of some sort, one suspects that it is to be used in "going to the water" *uwá:sv* ("by himself [or herself]").

2.

Now! Listen! Very quickly You have just come to hear!

You and I have just come to assemble the eyes from the meetingplaces of the Seven Clans.

>>

Then my body is not lonely: I, _____, am a very handsome man!

(My name is _____; my people are _____.)

When a spirit invoked is not named, the assumption
that the addressee is the Provider Himself is an almost
inevitable one.

The second line of the charm here is a felicitous way
of saying: "By means of Your assistance I have become
attractive to everybody."

The labeling of this *i:gawé:sdi* is significant: "To 'rebeautify' oneself; to 'remake' oneself." It does not mean
that if one uses the spell two processes, the one distinct
from the other, will take place, but rather that the one
process more or less equates with the other. However, if
one insists on being technical, this incantation is an *ado:-
du:hiso?dí:yi*. It formed a part of the collection mentioned
in Part I, No. 12.

3.

Now! Let us speak of beauty so that you will not look at
me with loneliness!

Although one cannot be absolutely sure as to the proper
classification of this jaunty little charm, a clue pointing
toward its purpose is in a footnote to it: "This is for a
woman. One spits upon one's hands." The symbolic washing of the face with a minute quantity of one's own saliva,
a substitute in an emergency for "going to the water," is
a motif in Cherokee magic that has previously been re-

ported (Kilpatrick, *The Sìquanìdʔ Dìl'tidégi Collection*, p. 5). This *i:gawé:sdi* would appear to be an "instant-*ado:-du:hisoʔdí:yi*," so to speak, something that would be of some small service when an unexpected meeting with a girl that the reciter wished to impress was imminent. Before using the charm the lover would empower it with his name, stated or thought, and possibly would also say the name of the girl.

This *i:gawé:sdi* comes from *Diga:dayo:sdí:i.*

4.

Now! I am as beautiful as the Red *Tsugv:tsala:la!*
(My clan is ————.)

I am as beautiful as the Red *Dla:nuwa!*
(My clan is ————.)

Now! I am as beautiful as the White Sun!
(My clan is ————.)

Without loneliness, I have just come to make my appearance!
I am a Little Man!

From the Cherokee point of view, the reciter is speaking of an ascending scale of spiritual powers: the dazzling and mysterious *Tsugv:tsala:la;* the enormous and fierce but radiant *Dhla:nuwa;* the Sun; a Son of Thunder. Here we have one of the numerous pieces of evidence that establish ranking in the spiritual hierarchy: even the members of the family of Thunder are assigned a superiority to the

Sun (cf. Part I, No. 8). As stated by a relator of one of the myths in Kilpatrick and Kilpatrick (*Friends of Thunder,* p. 137): "Thunder was the Ruler of the whole Universe"— by permission of the Provider Himself.

This uncaptioned *i:gawé:sdi,* an *ado:du:hiso?dí:yi* of rather conventional format and content, may be the text of a "going to the water" song. Stating the clan affiliation three times and the name not at all is a rhetorical device: "My clan is _____; yes, my clan is _____; my clan, to be sure, is _____; but as for my name —— well, that is Son of Thunder!"

This charm came from *Ado:lanv́:sdi Dé:ganugó:gv,* near Tahlequah, in Cherokee County.

5.

Now! I am as beautiful as the Red *Tsugv:tsala:la!*
All of you women are my possession.

From where my feet stand, on upward, I am beautiful.
I truly am a man!

From where my feet stand, upward, then, I am as beautiful
    as the very blossoms themselves!

I am as beautiful as the Red Rainbow!

"To sing in order to 'rebeautify' oneself for women" is the labeling of this virile little lyric. A charm of this type is generally considered to be most effective if sung in "going to the water," but it can be employed when and where needed, and it can be merely said (or thought) instead of being sung. Name and clan of the individual using it are announced before the four formal iterations of it.

The Rainbow is mentioned but, so far as we know, seldom or never invoked in erotic magic. It is met with rather frequently in Cherokee medicine, chiefly in connection with a condition called *gv:hnáge* ("the black").

The above song-text appears in a "medicine" book from *Gwagwó:hi*, a copy of an old manuscript from some community unknown to us, but probably in Mayes County. The medicine and magic of the northern part of the Cherokee country exhibit signs of deriving from some tradition that is unique.

6.

I am as beautiful as the *Dhla:nuwa!*

I am as beautiful as the Scarlet Tanager!

I am as beautiful as the *Tsugv:tsala:la!*

I am as beautiful as the Hummingbird!

Quite a number of laymen's "to 'rebeautify' oneself" *idi:gawé:sdi* fall into the stereotype wherein the incantator compares himself to a panel of four bird spirits or spirit birds. The scarlet tanager (*Piranga erythromelas*) and the hummingbird (*Archilochus colubris*) are often mentioned in such charms.

The above is from *Gha:hl(i)se:tsi Tso:dalv*. No explanation accompanies it. Our surmise is that it is a "going to

>>>

the water" song-text. A woman, as well as a man, might
use it.

7.

As beautiful as the Red Tobacco is, I am just as beautiful!

As beautiful as the Red *Dhla:nuwa* is, I am just as beautiful!

As beautiful as the Red Fishinghawk is, I am just as beautiful!

As beautiful as the Blue Tobacco is, I am just as beautiful!

The tobacco is both "Red," or success-producing, and
"Blue," or *uhí:soʔdí*-making.

The fishinghawk (*Pandion haliaetus carolinensis*) is
indeed a mighty Wizard throughout the whole range of
Cherokee mythology, medicine, and magic (cf. Mooney
and Olbrechts, *The Swimmer Manuscript*, pp. 265-67).
The assistance of this bird spirit in catching fish is of the
utmost value, and the medical duties of the fishinghawk,
observed in untranslated manuscripts, are numerous.

The notation upon this *Gha:hl(i)se:ts(i) Tso:dalv* charm
does not tell the whole story of the *i:gawé:sdi's* utility: "To
'remake' tobacco for a woman. This is also to acclimate
women"; for this is primarily *ado:du:hisoʔdí:yi* magic.

8.

As beautiful as is the Red Cardinal, I am beautiful!

As beautiful as is the Red *Dhla:nuwa*, I am beautiful!

As beautiful as is the Red Scarlet Tanager, I am beautiful!

As beautiful as is the Blue Cardinal, I am beautiful!

This is a variant of No. 6. The Cardinal (*Richmondena cardinalis*) is like the tobacco in the preceding example, first "Red" and then "Blue."

The caption upon this *Gha:hl(i)se:ts(i) Tso:dalv* charm says: "This also is another one to acclimate women," which it is; but it is to "rebeautify" oneself in order to do so.

9.

The Sparrow Hawk will be calling!
The Yellow Mockingbird will be calling!

Then I am as beautiful as the Bluebird!

I am as beautiful as the Hummingbird!

I am as beautiful as the Sea Gull!

The calling of the bird spirits, both of whom enjoy a high reputation for wizardry, may be a ritualistic reference to their magical prowess. "The Sparrow Hawk and the Yellow Mockingbird will be 'working' for me" is possibly the meaning contained in the two lines.

Gi:yági:yá, which we translate as "Sparrow Hawk," is a troublesome word; for it is by no means certain that the North Carolina and the Oklahoma Cherokees refer, or for that matter, ever referred to the same hawk by this term.

The caption to this *i:gawé:sdi*, from the same community as the three preceding examples, forthrightly says:

>>>

"For women." This incantation is seemingly a song-text.

10.

I am as beautiful as the Red Bird!

I am as beautiful as the Blue Bird!

I am as beautiful as the Yellow Bird!

Ha, then! I have just come to attach the eyes of all of you
to my body: "*Du! Du! Du! Du!*"

The Red Bird is not the Redbird, nor the Blue Bird
the Bluebird; it is an unspecified avian that changes colors.
The Cherokee word used is *tsi:sghwa*, the generic term
for a bird.

"*Du!*" is a rather protean onomatopoeia that can mean
many things. Here it probably signifies the attaching of the
admiring eyes: "Plop! Plop! Plop! Plop!"

Like the examples immediately preceding it, this un-
titled *ado:du:hiso?di:yi* might be a song-text. It is from
Se:lami:yi in southeastern Adair County, and is written in
the *Gi:dhahyó:hi* dialect.

11.

Now! I am as beautiful as the very blossoms themselves!

I am a man, you lovely ones, you women of the Seven
Clans!
(Now these are my people, ———, and this is my name,
———.)

Now! You women who reside among the Seven Peoples, I
have just come to intrude myself among you.

All of you have just come to gaze upon me alone, the most
   beautiful.

Now! You lovely women, already I just took your souls!

I am a man!
You women will live in the very middle of my soul.

Forever I will be as beautiful as the bright red blossoms!

    Clearly we deal in this instance with rather strong
"medicine." The fact that the text is septempartite is a
prima facie attestation to potency above the millrun. Its
directions confirm its authority: "This written is the utmost
for young men growing up to help themselves. To be said
four times. One is to blow upon finishing." In other words,
one merely says this "to 'rebeautify' oneself" incantation
four times, presumably at any convenient time or place,
and upon finishing each recitation one blows his breath
toward where the girl of his choice happens momentarily
to be.
    This rather pretty poem came from *Ghwo:lamí:i,* in
the extreme south of Muskogee County, an area that re-
tains today very little of its old Cherokee culture. Before
Oklahoma statehood it was in Canadian District of the
Cherokee Nation.

12.
Now! I am as beautiful as the Red Cardinal!

I can do as much as the Red Cardinal!

I am as much of a Wizard as the Red Cardinal!

I possess as much as the Cardinal!

One wonders why the "victorious" color (red) of the bird spirit is missing from the fourth line. Perhaps the *Gi:dhahyó:hi* medicine man who copied the charm inadvertently omitted a word.

This *i:gawé:sdi* is devoid of either title or directions. No matter how it may have been used in recent times, we hypothesize that originally it was a song-text for employment in an *ado:du:hiso?dí:yi* ritual wherein *wo:di* (paint) was applied to the body with the feather of a cardinal. This rite, chiefly enacted for the purpose of making a young man attractive to girls attending a dance, is seemingly now extinct, but detailed information concerning it has been recorded.

13.

(1)

In the very middle of the Morning Red I stand.
I am not lonely.
I am a man!

Ha! I have just sought quarry!
I am a Great Wizard!

The very Provider ever "remakes" me daily.

In my beauty I go about.
I walk in my splendor.

(2)

In the very middle of the Rainbow I stand.
I am not lonely.
I am a man!

Ha! I have just sought quarry!
I am a Great Wizard!

My Provider ever "remakes" me daily.

In my beauty I go about.

    The divergences of the second part of this *ado:dhlvhi:-so?dí:yi* from the first part are quantitatively smaller in the original Cherokee than in the translation. The scrupulous observance of these seemingly rather insignificant variations is, of course, deemed to be vital to the success of the incantation.

    The prescribed ritual, supplied verbally by the *Gi:-dhahyó:hi* shaman who gave the authors his personal copy of the text, is of much interest: The lover goes at earliest sunup to a flowing spring, faces east, says the *i:gawé:sdi* four times, and then washes his face. At a different spring he performs the same ritual the next morning; still another spring is visited upon the third successive morning, and upon the fourth morning he "works" at a fourth spring. Then upon the fifth morning he repairs to the spring which, of the four, is nearest his home and performs the rite once more.

    The motifs of four springs and a fifth performance superimposed upon a series of the usual four enactments of a ritual boldly dissonate with ordinary Cherokee magical practice. But then the Cherokees themselves recognize the speakers of the *Gi:dhahyó:hi* dialect, a fairly sizable segment of the tribe, as constituting a distinct social entity. While a superficial examination of their speech strongly suggests a South Carolinian origin for the *Gi:dhahyó:hi*-speaking people, they have a tradition that immediately preceding the Removal their ancestors were living in Wills Valley, in Alabama. Even at this late date, competent study of the *Gi:dhahyó:hi* people might prove to be ethnographically rewarding.

14.

Now! Red *Di:sdi!*
Ha, now! You have just come to "remake" my soul!

Now! You are a Great Wizard.

Now very quickly You have just come to open it.

Now! "Indeed he has just 'remade' himself!" I will be saying.

"Opening the soul" is a figure of speech that is infrequently seen in magical manuscripts. The verb "to open" (*-sdui:-*) is employed in everyday conversation in a manner quite similar to the way it is used in English—in reference to a door, or gate. And such is the case here.

The incantator is, of course, addressing himself when he says, "Indeed he has just 'remade' himself!" "I will be saying" is the very end to the closing line in hundreds of

Oklahoma medical conjurations (see Kilpatrick and Kilpatrick, "Cherokee Burn Conjurations," *Journal of the Graduate Research Center,* XXXIII, pp. 18, 20, 21), and in not a few North Carolina curing charms, but its appearance in magic is quite rare.

The above *i:gawé:sdi* appears in a *Gwagwó:hi* "medicine" book which is a rather recently made copy of an older manuscript that probably originated somewhere in the northern part of the Cherokee country. Its titling is: "To be said four times. To 'remake' oneself."

15.

Now! Ha! I alone am as beautiful as the Meadowlark!
(I am their only friend.)

I am alone in the Seven Clan Districts!
(I am their only friend.)

The Seven Eyes will be seeking me alone!
(I am their only friend.)

[My name is ————; my people are ————.]

The term in ancient Cherokee erotic magic that corresponds to the "boy friend" of modern American English is, surprisingly enough, "friend"; thus, "I am their only friend" equates with "I am the boy friend of them all." "I am alone in the Seven Clan Districts!" is an arch way of inferring that any young man other than the speaker stands a poor chance of being noticed by girls; "Seven Eyes" is seemingly a ritualism for "the eyes of all the young women

>>>

of the Seven Clans." The fact that in the aboriginal Cherokee society a young man had to marry a woman of one
of but two certain clans which were determined by his own
lineage (cf. Gilbert, "The Eastern Cherokees," Bureau of
American Ethnology, *Bulletin 133*, pp. 238-45) played no
part in love magic: a youth "rebeautified" or "remade" was
fascinating to all women.

Inasmuch as the above *i:gawé:sdi*, as written, is incom-
plete, we assume that a "name-clan" statement, such as we
have supplied, is improvised in order to fill out the form
of the charm.

The meadowlark (*Sturnella magna*) cuts a very small
figure in Cherokee magic, medicine, and mythology.

A note upon this incantation from *Tse:gí:i* is of con-
siderable interest: "To 'remake' oneself when going somewhere. Blow upon hands and chest four times." One might
amplify this somewhat laconic statement as follows: "Before going where girls are likely to be present, one can
make himself attractive to them by saying the above four
times, and by blowing one's breath upon one's hands and
chest after each recitation of the spell."

16.

Now! Hummingbird!

You and I are attired as one.

Ha! Very quickly when You and I conjure Your People and
mine are one, Your Heart and mine are one.

Now! You and I will be surpassingly beautiful, like the red,
red flowers!

The word for hummingbird here, *wa:lel(u)*, is a term applied to hummingbirds in general. While offhand we cannot recall a single instance of the hummingbird spirit's being invoked to perform a task pertaining to healing, for rather obvious reasons this lovely avian sprite appears with frequency in the white magic of eroticism.

Insofar as we can determine, this little *i:gawé:sdi* need merely be said. "To 'remake' oneself for women. To say four times" constitutes the note to it. We do not know the Cherokee settlement from which it came. The manuscript from which it was extracted is a contemporary copy of an older one.

17.

Listen!
(Ha, now! Very quickly She has just come to make Her
    appearance.)
You *Age:hyv Gu:ga!*
You have just brought Your Red Saliva to touch my body.
(My name is _____.)

The Blue One has just brought and hung out my Red
    Attire.
You have just come to "remake" me.

Without going by the Pathways of the _____ Clan Dis-
    trict, my footprints have just passed under them!
My motions will be tempting!

You woman, your name is _____; your people are the
_____.

>>>

There has always been a sustained communication between Eastern and Western Cherokees. The ethos of the medicine and magic of each of the two tribal divisions has been influenced by such factors as the emigration of individuals and small groups from Qualla and Snowbird Creek to the Cherokee Nation, and letters in Sequoyah syllabary dispatched from the Ozark foothills to coves in the Smokies.

If one had to pinpoint the exact quality that gives the North Carolina erotic incantation its distinctive flavor, one would probably conclude that it is its brooding, rhapsodic fervor. Western Cherokee love magic is full of light and air. Sometimes it is touchingly simple.

One does not have to take into account mechanical features, such as the characteristic opening "Listen! (*Sgeʔ!*)," in order to identify the foregoing *i:gawé:sdi* as North Carolinian (the ethnologists would say "Middle Cherokee," whatever that is): the very spirit of its poetry is North Carolinian.

The caption upon this incantation is "To 'remake' oneself," but by the text itself we are able to see that this is an understatement: the *i:gawé:sdi* is for the purpose of making oneself attractive to a woman who is named, while at the same time undermining the aspirations of a rival. In a remarkably imaginative flight, "The Blue One has just brought and hung out my Red Attire (My rival admits that my powers are greater than his)," the opponent is dealt with; a little later the helpful magical powers of his clansmen are clandestinely vitiated: "Without going by the Pathways of the _____ Clan District, my footprints have just passed under them!"

The footnote to the text says: "One is to 'work' at night.

Four times." Magic for a somewhat sinister purpose (in
this instance, to discomfit a rival) is sometimes enacted by
running water at midnight, not dawn. "Four times" means
"for four consecutive nights," although, of course, the
i:gawé:sdi is said four times at each "working."

This incantation came from *Gha:hl(i)se:ts(i) Tso:dalv.*

IV
ABASING

IV

ABASING

1.

Now! My name is _____.
My people are _____.

I originated in the Treetops.

Here in the roof of the dense forest my soul will be living
about.

Now! There where I surely enclosed you, surely will I be
enclosed!

    An explanation of the exact purpose of this exquisite
lyric is made difficult by the fact that a certain Cherokee
verb has no counterpart in English. In a general way the
myriad forms of this verb bear the implication that a
woman puts on high and mighty airs, and is given to
holding a suitor or husband as undesirable poor red trash.
A footnote says (and for the word "contemptuous" one
must substitute an understanding based upon the above):
"If someone is contemptuous, to make her turn back. To
be said four times."
    One might paraphrase this verse as follows: "My name
is _____, and my people are _____. My spirit is as
haughty and as free as yours; but the love with which I
surrounded you enslaves me as well as you."

Viewed aesthetically, the foregoing is the distillation of that which is so engaging in the ritualistic erotic literature of the Oklahoma Cherokees. Trenchant, epigrammatic, noble, constructed with a keen sense of form, it is a memorable miniature.

We are not certain as to the community from which this *i:gawé:sdi* came, but it was probably in Mayes County.

2.

Now!
Now, _____!
Ha! Without loneliness, I know the way you think!

My White Pathways go as far into the distance as those of
    the Cock.
"He:! He:! He:! He:! He:!"

As radiant as the Moon and the Stars, I have just alighted.
It is not in vain that I am capped with the crest of the
    Tsugv:tsala:la.
Without loneliness, I have just appeared.

I am a Red Man, a Great Wizard.
I go up there Above, and I return!

The term *tsadha:g(a) atsv:ya*, which we have translated as "Cock," nowadays has a restricted application to the male of the domestic chicken, but it would seem that in pre-Columbian times it was employed in reference to the male of some ground-dwelling fowl of the prairie chicken type. The word *tsadha:g(a)* is incorporated into place names. Note that the call of the fowl, imitated in the text, is not that of the barnyard rooster of the white man.

This beautiful *i:gawé:sdi*—"For a woman, if she is scornful"—glows with some delightful phraseology. "My White Pathways go as far into the distance as those of the Cock" is a matchless assertion of masculinity; and while the line "As radiant as the Moon and the Stars, I have just alighted" might be equated with an extract from the works of some European second-class master, "It is not in vain that I am capped with the crest of the *Tsugv:tsala:la*" is a line that was turned with a fine frenzy.

"I go up there Above, and I return" expresses with astonishing concision the supernatural gift.

Apparently this incantation, found under the circumstances related in Part I, No. 12, has no adjunctive ritual.

3.

He-wa-hi!
He-wa-hi!
He-wa-hi!
He-wa-hi!

Your soul stands about over there.
In loneliness it stands about over there.

But the White Pathway lies before me.
Over there where I turned myself over, let your soul go
    underneath!

This is your name: _____.
Your people are _____.

"Merely to sing if a woman pretends to be superior [*u:dli yatsé:lv:sgá*]" is the caption upon this incantation from *Gwagwó:hi,* but manifestly only the opening is to be sung. The syllables *"He-wa-hi!"* may not be meaningless, as upon a cursory inspection they would appear to be; for, as is frequently the case with Cherokee song-texts, they may be a fusion of several words. One possibility is this: *"HiɁaɁ hegwo:hi* [Here is a big one: you]!"

The gist of the meaning in this *i:gawé:sdi* is something akin to this: "It is your soul, not mine, that is going to be lonely. My future is assured. Inasmuch as I have taken a new grip upon myself, you are the one that is going to capitulate."

4.

Now! Listen!
You Little Man!

Now very quickly the Black Tobacco has just come to
    strike you.
(This is your name: _____.
This is my name: _____.)

Now! The White Pathways are mine.
I am attired.

Yellow Mockingbird, there is fire in my soul!
It just descended into the very middle of your heart!

"If a woman scorns you. To 'remake' tobacco" is the labeling of this rather pretty *i:gawé:sdi* that was found scribbled in a diminutive pocket notebook from *Yuwa:sí:i*, in Delaware County. Its last two lines are rather striking, although, to be sure, all the rest of it is composed of clichés.

5.

Now! Listen!
Bluebird!
Very quickly You have just come to hear.
Ha, then! Ha! You are a Great Wizard.
In all things You do not fail.
Ha, Then! Let the White Pathways lie before one.

Ha, then! The Sparrow Hawk has just come to pierce the
    very middle of your soul.
Now He has just come to place there something lonely.

Then the Goldfinch has just brought loneliness to you alone.
(Then He was a Great Wizard.
He just came to bring her Blue Worms.)

You and I will be following the Pathways.
Ha, then! He was a Great Wizard!

Rather frequently one runs across an *i:gawé:sdi* that will have incorporated in the directions for its use the personal endorsement of the individual who wrote it down. Accompanying this incantation from *Gha:hl(i)se:ts(i) Tso:-dalv* is a note saying: "To use when a woman ridicules you, and if she pretends to scorn you. This is what I use. One uses tobacco."

>>>

The figure of the Sparrow Hawk flying in to pierce with his fierce beak a hole in the hard heart of the woman in order to place therein a regret is a forceful one. The word *ts(i)sgo:ya* is used in reference to all sorts of creeping and wriggling little grubs and larvae. It is such that the Goldfinch (*Spinus tristis tristis*) brings to trouble the conscience of the woman.

What the Bluebird spirit does is not clear. Perhaps he exercises a supervisory authority over the entire procedure of getting the incantator and his snobbish girl friend back to "following the Pathways."

6.

Now this is my name: _____.
Ha, then! These are my people: _____.

I just requested that _____.
It has just come to befall you.

Then loneliness, _____, has just come to smite your soul.
It was just decided that this will be your fate, night and
    day, until the White Pathways lying before you fade
    away.

My name is _____.
You are thinking of me, _____!

In a sense the above is, of course, an *uhi:so?dí* incantation, but its caption makes it clear that it possesses a special utility: "This is to prepare tobacco for someone who habitually scorns one." The third line exhibits a curious tech-

nical innovation: a blank wherein one may improvise a
specific ill that he wishes to descend upon the head of his
uppish wife or sweetheart. (And we would like to point
out that there is nothing to prevent a woman from using
this *i:gawé:sdi* upon a man whose self-esteem has become
intolerable.)

The sixth line is of surpassing loveliness. Although its
timbre is peculiarly Cherokeean, it would grace the work
of any poet in any culture.

This masterfully constructed lyric is from *Gi:dhahyó:hi.*

7.

Now! As beautiful as the *Tsugv:tsala:la,* I have just come
    to stand before you.
This, you woman, is your clan: _____.
This is your name: _____.

Now! You will not be able to remove your gaze from me.
My body, down to the standing of my feet, will be con-
    tinually anointed with your blood and your saliva.

Truly you will never be able to forget.

Your soul and mine will ever be inside of each other.
Your flesh and mine will become one for as long as Time
endures!

One discovers here and there texts that achieve a pas-
sionate intensity without sacrifice of the elevation that is
inherent in the style of the erotic *idi:gawé:sdi.* One feels
here something of the same spirit that abides in the typical

European love lyric. The approach here is personal; the entire text is delivered to an individual, even though the recipient is not corporally present. No supernatural helper is petitioned.

The identification upon this *Gwagwó:hi* incantation reads: "For a woman if she scorns one. To remake cut twist tobacco. One is to finish it four times." The content of the text would strongly suggest that one could use the *i:gawé:-sdi* for the general purpose of what the Cherokees call "imprisoning" or "acclimating" a woman (see Part V, following).

V
RETAINING AFFECTION

V

RETAINING AFFECTION

1.

I have "remade" myself with the very *Age:hyv Gu:gv* Herself, you woman!

(This is your name: _____.)

I will change you into a mere dog.

You will be yelping behind me as I go: "*GhaℙΙ GhaℙΙ GhaℙΙ GhaℙΙ*"

In everyday conversation the verb *-atse:lv:-* has the force of "to pretend," "to dissimulate," or "to put on airs," but in a ritualistic context it is often used to express the concept of the metamorphosis of a being from human form to animal or avian form. Thus, as the verb is used above, a woman is "pretended" into being a dog.

The scant published evidence that is available would give one the impression that the dog is mentioned far more frequently in the rituals of North Carolina than in those of Oklahoma (cf. Mooney, "Sacred Formulas," pp. 345-49; Mooney and Olbrechts, *The Swimmer Manuscript,* 271-73, 279-81). Among the Western Cherokees the ceremonial role of the dog is principally that as a symbol for constancy in love; the dog spirit is somewhat infrequently invoked.

Cherokee oldsters still remember the aboriginal tribal

dog, a semi-sleek, wolfish beast with a dark spot over each
eye. As late as thirty or forty years ago many of the dogs
seen in the yards of cabins in the Cherokee Hills still
clearly showed their ancestry. The white people called
these animals "kanutchee dogs," a name derived from *gá:-
nvts(i),* a hickory nut and hominy soup which is the Cherokee national dish.

"To remake tobacco for a woman" is the rather unin-
formative title of this *gala:n(i)sdoʔdi* from *Tse:gí:i.* The
date of the writing down of the *i:gawé:sdi* is supplied:
February 21, 1933.

2.

Now! Listen!
My Provider!

I have a small dog.
I possess her forever.

Always she will sleep upon my body.

"*Waʔ! Waʔ! Woʔ! Waʔ! Woʔ!*" you will be saying as you
  will be walking behind me.

The imitation of the cries of animals and the calls of
birds in *idi:gawé:sdi* is worthy of a whole study unto itself.
Here one observes that the text says, "I have a small dog,"
or, in other words, a puppy. The syllables in the last line
constitute a remarkably faithful reproduction of the sharp
and happy barking of a playful young dog.

This *Gwagwó:hi* incantation is labeled: "To acclimate

a woman." Very likely it may be merely said, or used as a tobacco-"remaker" at the option of its user.

3.

Quickly think of me, you woman, not of the other man!
I am not lonely.

Just as one owns a dog, I own you.
I am not lonely.

Your Pathway and mine to the White—Seven!—Resting-
place is one.
I am not lonely. Seven!

Your soul moves about in loneliness.

You are not to think away to the soul of the Blue One.

I am just like a dog.

"*Ya?! Wo?! Ya?! Wo?!*" I will be saying.

In this *gala:n(i)sdo?di* the incantator compares himself to a dog, one with a more mature, deeper-sounding bark than that in the preceding specimen, a dog that will relent-lessly track down its quarry, the love of a woman. In one sense, this uncaptioned *i:gawé:sdi* from *Gi:dhahyó:hi* is an *uhí:so?dí*-producer; many incantations fall into several classifications simultaneously.

One notes that whoever wrote this septempartite text down took the trouble to insert the interpolations of the strengthening sacred numeral that he employed when he recited the incantation. One assumes that this *i:gawé:sdi* is effective either as a tobacco-"remaker" or a self-contained charm.

4.

Now! Listen!
Ha! Who are you?
The name, you woman!

Ha! Very quickly the Little White Dog has just come to romp with your soul.

Ha! He has just come to place my body against it.

You can do nothing about it!

Chewing tobacco can be remade with about as much facility as can smoking tobacco; in fact, magically infused chewing tobacco formerly was much relied upon as an aid in gambling and in athletic contests. We see from the directions upon the engaging little charm above that a quid has its place in the game of love: "Tobacco is put into the mouth. One blows upon her breast and neck. This written is for women."

Mooney ("Sacred Formulas," pp. 380-81) records the North Carolina ceremony whereby a newly married husband fixes the affections of his wife by an appropriate incantation accompanied by the rubbing of his saliva upon her breast while she is asleep. This *Gha:hl(i)se:ts(i) Tso:-dalv i:gawé:sdi* is for remaking tobacco to be used for a similar purpose: a minute bit of it is blown upon the back of the neck and the breast of a sweetheart or wife whose fidelity a man wishes to retain.

5.

Ya-ne-hi!
Ya-ne-hi!
Ya-ne-hi!
Ya-ne-hi!

Like a dog, you will be standing right behind where I am
    standing. Seven!
For I am a White Man.

Like a dog, you will be standing right behind where I am
    standing. Seven!
Your thoughts will be aching.

Just like a dog, you will be standing right behind me.
Your thoughts will be lonely. Seven!

Just like a dog, you will be standing behind me.

    The prefatory syllables—to be sung, no doubt—may derive from *ané:hi* ("residers, they"), possibly an allusion to the household of the incantator.
    This text from *Gha:hl(i)se:ts(i) Tso:dalv* is annotated as follows: "To 'remake' tobacco. To be prepared in the morning [at dawn, by running water], or just anytime. Then for women it is to be smoked three times per day." The three times for smoking the tobacco and blowing its

smoke upon or toward the wife or lover would be at dawn, at noon, and at dusk.

As in No. 3, interpolations are written into the text.

6.

I just consumed your soul!

I just consumed your flesh!

I just consumed your saliva!

Grasp what I possess!

The *gala:n(i)sdoꞏdi* ritual reported by Mooney (see No. 4) opens with a song, the lines of which are sung in succession, each one four times, for four nights. (Mooney's translation of it contains an error of no great consequence: the word *tsigi* is not "I take," but "I just took"):

     —Your spittle, I take, I eat it.
     —Your body, I take, I eat it.
     —Your flesh, I take, I eat it.
     —Your heart, I take, I eat it.

There exist a good many Oklahoma charms for the same purpose that at first glance give the appearance of being paraphrases of the North Carolina text. In Oklahoma, however, they are usually said, not sung, and they stand as independent entities. We do not accept this as evidence of ritualistic decay; it is a case of parallel streams of tradition. The Oklahoma examples are fully as old as that of Mooney. The concept, cherished by anthropologists, that the ritualism of North Carolina has been more resistant than that of Oklahoma stems from a lack of knowledge of both.

There is no caption upon this specimen from *Dhlv:-datsí:i.*

7.

Now! Ha! Very quickly I have just come to take away your heart.

Ha! Very quickly I have just come to take away your thought.

Ha! Very quickly I have just come to take away your breath.

Ha! Very quickly I have just come to take away your saliva.

In a general way the qualities that the husband professes to purloin are arranged in what to the mind of the Cherokee traditionalist is an ascending gamut of values. Most but not all *idi:gawé:sdi* of this genre place the saliva last.

The above example is to be delivered *in toto* four times, not a line at a time.

In the manuscript from *Gha:hl(i)se:ts(i) Tso:dalv* we are informed that the incantation is: "To imprison a woman with."

>>>

8.

Now! Ha! Quickly I have just come to take away your
   heart.

Ha! Quickly I have just come to take away your breath.

Ha! Quickly I have just come to take away your saliva.

Ha! Quickly I have just come to take away your blood.

For some reason (a copyist's error?) the saliva is listed
next to last here, not last; otherwise the *i:gawé:sdi* is
a variant, possessing no particular intrinsic interest, of
No. 7.

The purpose of the charm, from *Gi:dhahyó:hi,* is stated
to be: "To acclimate a woman with."

9.

I am as Red, as beautiful as the Rainbow.

Your heart has just been taken by me.

Your blood has been taken by me.

Your flesh has been taken by me.

Your eyes have been taken by me.

Your saliva has been taken by me.

Your saliva and mine are one forever.
You are a Wizard!

Inasmuch as no spirit is called upon anywhere in the text, we assume that the terminal line is self-addressed. Needless to say, it is customary to say or to think the name of the individual toward whom the incantation is directed preparatory to beginning the standard four deliveries of the charm. *Idi:gawé:sdi* of this type are held to be fully as effective when employed by a female as when used by a male.

This unlabeled specimen, written upon a loose sheet of paper, is from *Se:lamí:yi.*

10.

Now! Your saliva was just taken by me.

Your saliva and mine will now be as one, one assumes.

Now! Your soul was now just taken from your heart by me.

Your soul and mine will now be as one, one assumes.

The ritual that ordinarily accompanies this *i:gawé:sdi*, as well as Nos. 6-9, is quite simple, and different from the North Carolina procedure as reported by Mooney (see No. 4): After the spouse or lover says the text *sotto voce*, or thinks it, he surreptitiously blows his breath gently upon the breast of the woman whose affection he wishes to make permanent. If the woman is at a distance, he blows his breath toward her.

The above incantation, from *Ado:lanv̀:sdi Dé:ganugó:- gv*, has no caption.

11.

There is no loneliness in the Seven Clan Districts.

He and I have just decreed Darkness for you, so that you
    will not be able to see the Blue One.
He stated that while you live you will be unable to bring
    your gaze elsewhere other than upon my body.

The Blue One is not to live there in your soul.
He just relinquished his hold upon it.

You are not to let your thoughts wander!

    To be sure, this *i:gawé:sdi* contains its share of stock
verbiage; yet as a whole it possesses literary merit. Several
of its lines rise above the ordinary, and its construction is
craftsmanlike.

    The "He" who has assisted in blinding the woman to
the qualifications of a rival, the "Blue One," is probably
the Provider.

    For its origin, see Part I, No. 12. "To prepare tobacco
to acclimate a woman" is its identification.

12.

Now! Ha! Take it!
Quickly, *Tsugv:tsala:la*, You have just come to hear.
Ha! You have just come to take her soul.
(Her name is _____.)

(Then very quickly They have just come to live with my
    soul!)

Now! Red Spider! Very quickly You have just come to tie
up her soul.
Ho:! Put it in the White Chair in which she is sitting dining.

You will be thinking of me alone!

There is a special subclass of *gala:n(i)sdoʔdi idi:gawé:-
sdi* for the "conjuring" of a wife's place at the dining table
in order to make the woman content with her homelife.
One of these charms is said in her absence over a plate
from which she will later eat. A bowl or a dish from which
a newly acquired domestic animal eats similarly can be
"conjured" for the purpose of making the beast happy with
its new environment.

"They" in the fifth line refers to the spirits, the *Tsugv:-
tsala:la* and the Red Spider.

The explanation accompanying this example, from
Gha:hl(i)se:ts(i) Tso:dalv, says: "To say at the dining table
when one wishes for her to be acclimated. To say at the
dining table where her dish is."

13.

In the White House, my Resting-place, you did not just
    become lonely, ———.
It is there that your soul will be filled with love.
Your thought will not wander.

The White Food is mine.
You did not just become lonely.
Your soul will be filled with love at last.

〉〉〉

In my White Resting-place you did not just become lonely.
Finally there your soul will be filled with love at last.

Our two souls will be continually meeting while passing
    back and forth.

Technical devices, some of them exceedingly subtle, by
which *idi:gawé:sdi* are unified are oftentimes distorted or
lost in translation. In this grave and tender lyric, however,
certain of the structural pins still stand forth to the view.
If one assigns letters to motifs as follows: A, "White"; B,
"Resting-place"; C, ". . . you did not just become lonely";
D, ". . . filled with love," the rondo-like repetitive scheme
would present this graphic aspect:

Line	*Motif*
1	A B C
2	D
3	____
4	A
5	C
6	D
7	A B C
8	D
9	____

The titling of this *Tse:gí:i* text is somewhat misleading:
"To say four times to remake tobacco to smoke if a woman
scorns one"; for while indeed the *i:gawé:sdi* can be used
for the purpose stated, it is a typical *gala:n(i)sdoʔdi.*

VI
SEPARATING

VI

SEPARATING

1.

Now! You Two White Persons!

You, _____, are a lonely man.

Pass on toward the Nightland!

Your two souls are not to behold each other again.

Now quickly another man just come to strike in the very middle of your soul!

Ha, then! The Seven Thunderers glitter all about me!

I am a Red Man!

This venomous little *di:dagale:n(v)dho?dí:yi,* molded in true septempartite form for all of its diminutive size, is from *Dhlv:datsí:i,* in Adair County. Its titling indicates that it serves a special purpose: "To break them up if they are friends."

We doubt that the "Two White Persons" are the Sons of Thunder in a "white" (blissful) aspect; one would expect them to be "red" (powerful), or "blue" (trouble-bringing) in the roles that they would play for their invoker. It is probably the happy and unsuspecting lovers

123

>>>

who are being addressed. The girl, oddly enough, is not
named, as is her boy friend; she is merely told that her
lover is going to be replaced. The magician infers that inti-
mate association with members of the Family of Thunder
has invested him with Thunder-like attributes.

In all likelihood the above is an example of what
the Cherokees call a *yi:gawé:sdigwú*, an incantation that
one simply says four times without any adjunctive ritual
whatsoever. Needless to say, this is a medicine man's professional spell, as are all *di:dagale:n(v)dhoʔdí:yi* incantations.

2.

Their souls: _____, _____!
Now! Listen!
Black Diamondback Rattlesnake!
Quickly You have just come to hear.
You are a Great Wizard, and a failer in nothing.

Now quickly You float into the Place of Peace of the Red
    Water in the very middle of the House!

Now! Listen!
Blue Velvettail Rattlesnake!
Quickly You have just come to hear.
You are a Great Wizard, and a failer in nothing.

Then quickly You have just come to untie their souls where
    their White Pathway lies!

Although this *di:dagale:n(v)dhoʔdí:yi*, from the same

community as the preceding example, is captioned: "To separate lovers or mates," like the other specimen it is clearly primarily for a restricted purpose, to undermine a marriage, and it, too, need but be said.

The ornate sixth line must mean something approximating this: "You quickly spoil a successful marital relationship." That line that formally matches this, the final one, is rather striking, and might be paraphrased thusly: "You have just come to separate them in the midst of their happiness."

The opening that identifies the victims is quite out of the ordinary.

3.

Now! Red Ants!
Ha! Very quickly!
(These are his [or her] people: _____; this is his [or her] name: _____.)

In the very middle of his [or her] very soul all of You have
    just come down.
All of You have just come to make war.

Ha, then! All of You Ants will be Great Wizards!
Ha, then! In the very middle of his [or her] soul They have
    just come to flog with Red Thongs!

These Red Ants are not the large venomous insects whose hills dot the landscape of the American Southwest. The designation used is for ants of any sort, arrayed in the hue of "success."

⟫⟫

This incantation is for the purpose of arousing animosity in an individual against his or her mate, lover, or platonic friend. The other member of the pair is untouched by magic per se, but, of course, suffers from the supernaturally induced hatred of the bewitched companion. As *di:dagale:n(v)dho?dí:yi* incantations go, this is a rather bland one. In fact, technically speaking, it is not primarily a "separator," although the end product of its use may be the same as if it were one; it is to sow discord. It can be used by a layman, if he knows it, to get revenge for being jilted or insulted, or for any other cause. There exist *idi:-gawé:sdi* of this type specifically useful in creating "a small amount of anger."

The explanatory note to this incantation from *Gwa-gwó:hi* reads: "One is to say it four complete times. To prepare tobacco."

4.

The Red Snapping Turtle has just come to perform.
He has just come to rest on the other side of the Nightland.
He has just come to rot!

You Two Little Men are Great Wizards.
You Two fail in nothing.
Very quickly I have just come to let You Two hear the
   Word.

Very quickly, _____, I have just come to put the Red
   Knife in your right hand!

Very quickly, _____, I have just come to put the Red
   Stick in your left hand!

We deal here with a far more potent "anger-maker" than the preceding specimen, and if the incantator chooses to do so, he can boost its power; for the note to it states: "This is to make people angry. To remake tobacco four days. If in a hurry, fast all day. Friends or mates." What is meant here is this: If the incantator wishes to accelerate the taking effect of the spell, and also to render it more devastating, he may elect to fast all day following his fourth "working" at the water at dawn. This is generally done when performing magic to take human life.

"The Nightland" is the symbol of destruction, oblivion, death. "The other side of the Nightland" typifies the utter negation of happiness, of love and life.

The "Two Little Men" are the Sons of Thunder.

The Red Knife of strife is figuratively placed in the right hand of the male of the pair of mates or lovers against whom the incantator is "working." The name of the victim is inserted at the place provided for it. The Red Stick of discord is held by the left hand of the female, who is likewise identified by name.

The above *i:gawé:sdi* appears in a manuscript that was probably written at *Gha:hl(i)se:ts(i) Tso:dalv.*

5.

Now! Listen!
Now quickly, Blue Sparrow Hawk, from Your Place of
    Peace Above You have just come to hear.
You are to take the Blue Tobacco.

Ha! The Blue Tobacco has just come to let you hear.
We have just come to make it rise.

Ha! You have just descended the Pathway, _____!

Ha! You and I have just come to make sport of their souls.

Blue Tobacco, You have just descended.
We have just made heavy the soul that He has just come
   to eye.

You have just come to chop them.
You and I will place them in the very middle of my breast
   where I, entirely Red, stand in the Sunland.

I, _____, am not lonely—Ha!—in the various Clan Districts!

Inasmuch as this text is in seven sections, and not the
more conventional four, clearly we are in the presence of
strong magic. The footnote to it bears this out; for, as in
connection with the preceding example, fasting is prescribed: "To remake tobacco. Arise early in the morning,
four days. To break up sweethearts or friends. Fast all
day."

It is evident that most of the sorcery is focused upon an
individual. Cherokee verb-forms differentiate you (singu-
lar), you (dual), and you (plural). "The Blue Tobacco
has just come to let you [singular] hear [i.e., to exercise its
power upon you]" is seen in one line; "You [singular] have
just descended the Pathway, _____ [i.e., Your fate has
just taken a downward turn]" in another one.

It is the Blue Sparrow Hawk who is "to take the Blue
Tobacco," i.e., to convey the enchanted tobacco smoke to

its victims; the joint efforts of the incantator and the bird spirit are going to "make it rise," i.e., indue it with supernatural qualities. Presumably it is also the Blue Sparrow Hawk who fastens a fierce eye upon the bewitched soul, and who helps the sorcerer hew into the bonds that unite victim and partner.

This *Gha:hl(i)se:ts(i) Tso:dalv* incantation is indubitably for the purpose of eliminating the male of a pair of individuals so that the magican may have a chance at the favors of the female. The wonderful penultimate line, woven of pure poetry, is positive proof; for in mundane language it says: "You, Blue Sparrow Hawk, and I will place the sorry ruin of their union in my heart, where the only thing left alive in the wreckage, the love of the woman, will remain; for I shall be totally victorious."

6.

Ha! White Sparrow Hawk!
You live Above.
You have just come to scream: "Your soul has just been
    separated!"

Ha! Blue Mourning Dove!
You live Above.
You have just come to call: "Ha! Your soul has just been
    separated!"

Ha! The White Pathway has just been divided.
Loneliness itself will be breaking your two souls along the
    Valley.

The Pathway which is White has just parted in the very
middle!

The White Sparrow Hawk addresses the male, the Blue
Mourning Dove speaks to the female of the pair that is
being subjected to sorcery. The names of the victims are
either announced before the incantation is begun, or else
they are inserted after the words "Your soul" in lines 3
and 6.

The "White Pathway" that has just been divided and
which has "just parted in the very middle" is, quite obviously, the serene course of friendship, courtship, or marriage.

The word "Separator" is the only label upon this *i:ga-
wé:sdi* from *Gha:hl(i)se:ts(i) Tso:dalv*. It does not appear
to be for use in "remaking" tobacco. Seemingly, it is merely
to be said four times.

7.

(1)

Now! There in the middle of the Above rise up, Black
Barred Owl!
Remove Your Attire!
Bring it down!

Ha, now! You two are to be enclosed in loneliness, He
stated.
As one the Pathways of you two will be lying before you.
As one your two souls will be yoked together in the very
middle of the Light.
Ha! The Pathways of you two will be lying before you.

Your Blue Saliva will be dropping before you, _____,
    where the Pathway to the Nightland is waiting!

Ha! This is my clan: _____.

(2)

Now! Listen! Ha! In the very middle of the Above rise up,
    Black Sparrow Hawk!
Remove Your Attire!
Bring it down!

These, _____, are your people.

Ha! As one—Ha!—you two will be enclosed.
Ha! As one the Pathways of you two will be lying before
    you.
Ha! As one your two souls will be yoked together.
(These are your people: _____; this is your name:
    _____.)

Ha! In the very middle of the Light, "Your soul is dis-
    traught!" He has just come to say!

As is the case in many another separator, the first part
of this black-hued *i:gawé:sdi* is directed toward the male
of a pair of lovers or mates, the second part toward the
female. The Black Barred Owl is directed to remove his
sepulchral attire and to wrap the one in its gloom; the
Black Sparrow Hawk is enjoined to perform a similar dis-
service for the other. Both victims, bound together in
misery that is open to the inspection of all who know them,

are sent down the trail where death waits for one, suffering
for the other.

Calling attention to the blazing expressive power in
the line, "Your Blue Saliva will be dropping before you,
_____, where the Pathway to the Nightland is wait-
ing!" is but the pointing out of but a detail in what as a
whole makes for uncommonly forceful verbal craftsman-
ship.

"To remake tobacco to smoke to separate persons, to
smoke where they live" is the statement of the purpose of
this *Gha:hl(i)se:ts(i) Tso:dalv* incantation.

8.

Now! Eagle!
You have just flown in!
(This is what he is named: _____.)
You have just alighted in the middle of his soul.
Night has just arrived in his soul.

He says that He has just come to put the Black Spoon in
    her hand.
She will not see it.

Their souls have just come under the very middle of the
    Briar-patch.
They will not see it.

"Ghwa:! Ghwa:! Da:sd(a)!"

The Spoon stands here as the symbol of the domestic
status of the woman of the pair against whom this incanta-

tion is projected. The Eagle spirit, who brings gloom to the existence of the husband, secretly brings hate to the heart of the wife and puts "the Black Spoon in her hand." The marital relationship of both, through some cause that neither understands, becomes a thing of wounds and pain, a "Briar-patch."

"*Ghwa:! Ghwa:!*" is the cry of the Eagle; "*Da:sd(a)!*" is a thunderclap—additional evidence, perhaps, of the Eagle's role as Thunder's emissary.

"To remake tobacco or merely to say to separate them. Four times" is the subscript. The *i:gawé:sdi* is from *Tse:gí:i* or *Dhlv:datsí:i*.

9.

Now! Listen!
Red Raven!
Very quickly You have just come to hear.
Your Place of Peace is Above.
You fail in nothing.

Very quickly You have just come to bring down the Red
    Tobacco, a Great Wizard.
"*Ghwa:!*"
You have just come to put it under the soul of _____.
The Red Tobacco is a Great Wizard.

Ha! Without resting, his Pathway has just turned toward
    the Nightland.
Ha! He is not to turn back anywhere.
Truly somewhere his soul is to be broken!

"Ghwa:!"
The Red Tobacco has just come to cover his soul!
"Ghwa:! Wa:hl(a)!"

The caption upon this text from *Ghwo:lamí:i,* in Muskogee County, is a mite misleading; for while the incantation indubitably is for the purpose stated: "This is to 're-make' tobacco to break up married persons, and also even to kill them," it is so constructed as to deal with but one mate at a time. But not a word need be changed should the sorcerer, after having given his attention to one of a pair, decide to hurl this same curse after the other. In Cherokee "his Pathway" and "his soul" are identical with "her Pathway" and "her soul."

"Ghwa:!" quite obviously is the call of the "Red," all-powerful Raven; *"Wa:hl(a)!"* is a rumble of thunder.

10.

Now! Listen!
Red Velvettail Rattlesnake!
Ha! Now quickly You have just come to hear.
You fail in nothing.

Ha! Where their souls meet—Seven!—quickly You have just
    come to break—Ha!—without their knowing it!

Listen!
Red Panther!
Ha! Now very quickly You have just come to hear.
You fail in nothing.

Ha! Where their souls meet, quickly You have just come
   to break—Seven! Ha!—without their knowing it!
You have just come to spit!
Ha! You are very angry!

The spirits of various species of rattlesnakes are often
called upon in *di:dale:n(v)dho?di:yi* magic, that of the
panther but rarely. The latter, in fact, is very weakly rep-
resented in erotic *idi:gawé:sdi*. His figure looms large
in other categories of Cherokee magic, however—notably
those for assistance in fighting, and for protection.

The spirits in the foregoing join forces to perform a
common duty: to break apart the fusion of a pair of individuals at the point "where their souls meet."

One will notice that two interpolations are written in.

This incantation is from *Gha:hl(i)se:ts(i) Tso:dalv;* its
purpose: "To 'remake' tobacco. To prepare it in the morning to be smoked during the day. This which is written is
a separator to separate them."

11.

(1)

Red Cardinal!
"Quickly I have just come to hear!"

He and I have just come to "remake" the Red Tobacco.
He and I have just come to shake your soul.

This is your name: _____.
You have no people.

It has become known that these are my people: _____,
    and that this is my name: _____.

(2)

Blue Cardinal!
"Quickly I have just come to hear!"

He and I have just come to "remake" the Blue Tobacco.
He and I have just come to shake your soul.

This is your name: _____.
You have no people.

It has become known that these are my people: _____,
    and that this is my name: _____.

(3)

You White Cardinal!
"Quickly I have just come to hear!"

He and I have just come to "remake" the White Tobacco.
He and I have just come to shake your soul.

This is your name: _____.
You have no people.

It has become known that these are my people: _____,
    and that this is my name: _____.

(4)

Yellow Cardinal!

"Quickly I have just come to hear!"

He and I have just come to "remake" the Yellow Tobacco.
He and I have just come to shake your soul.

This is your name: _____.
You have no people.

It has become known that these are my people: _____,
and that this is my name:_____.

The line, "You have no people," is one for which we
have no ready exegesis. One possibility is that we have here
an incantation specifically designed for use against a member of some social group other than the Cherokees. Such a
person would, of course, within the Cherokee frame of
reference have no clan. Any incantation designed for such
a purpose would of necessity be post-Columbian, and there
exists a flavor of modernity in this one. Another possibility
is that we have here magic tailor-made for a clanless
Cherokee, one whose mother, or whose mother's mother,
for example, was not a Cherokee. A third possibility is that
this *i:gawé:sdi* is a weapon against an individual whose
clan affiliation is simply not known to the magician, and
the clanless status of that person is a ritualistic posture.
    Note the sly deviation from the repeat-pattern in the
statement of the color of the White Cardinal. In Cherokee
the mutation of "White" to "You White" is effected by the
substitution of the syllable *tsa* for the syllable *u*. The failure
to honor this alteration would nullify the force of the incantation.

The text is from *Gha:hl(i)se:ts(i) Tso:dalv;* its purpose
is defined as: "This which is written is to separate them."
It is for "remaking" tobacco.

12.

(1)

You Two Men!
You Two Men!
You Two Men!
You Two Men!

You Two are Great Wizards.
The Place of Peace of You Two is Above.

Very quickly He has just come to hear.

Very quickly You Two have just come to "remake" the
    Red Tobacco.

(2)

You Two Men!
You Two Men!
You Two Men!
You Two Men!

You Two are Great Wizards.
Very quickly You Two have just come to "remake" the
    Black Tobacco.
(These are their names: —————, —————.)

He has just come to lay it in the very middle of their souls.

Now it has become necessary for them to be separated.

The "You Two Men!" which opens each section may be sung.

The "He" in the line "Very quickly He has just come to hear" is one of the Sons of Thunder; the "He" in the line "He has just come to lay it in the very middle of their souls," is the other one.

The above *Gha:hl(i)se:ts(i) Tso:dalv* incantation, as one may see in the directions following, is for "remaking" chewing tobacco which, masticated and mixed with the saliva of the incantator, is expectorated about the entrances to the house of the victims so that unwittingly they will come into contact with it: "This written is to separate them. This tobacco one uses if going near their home. Now one bit of tobacco is put into the mouth."

13.
Now! Very quickly pillow your head upon the Soul of the
    Dog, outside, where there is loneliness!

(Your name is _____.)

In the very middle of your two bodies loneliness has just
    come to think.

You are to be broken in the Pathway.

Now! Where the joining is has just come to be divided.

Your two souls have just come to be divided somewhere in
    the Valley.

>>>

Without breaking your soul, I have just come to stupefy
you with the Smoke of the Blue Tobacco.

Short, but septempartite and therefore uncommonly
devastating, this finely wrought *di:dagale:n(v)dhoɁdi:yi*
contains some memorable creative flights. The images of
the desolation of the soul of the doomed spouse, who is
ejected from home in opprobrium, and of the misery that
comes to brood in the inmost beings of the mates are indeed superb.

"You are to be broken in the Pathway" and the final
line are both addressed to whichever mate, husband or
wife, is the principal target.

"This written is to 'remake' tobacco to separate them"
is the caption of the *Gha:hl(i)se:ts(i) Tso:dalv i:gawé:sdi.*

VII
MISCELLANEOUS

VII

MISCELLANEOUS

1.

Now! Listen!
Ha! Look at me and think that I am beautiful.

Ha! Look at me and think that I am not lonely.

Ha! Let us speak of beauty.

Now! Ha, then! He will not take it away!
(My name is _____.
My people are _____.)

We see here the text of a song for "remaking" a comb. It can be used by a woman, although the directions to it read: "For women. One goes to the water, washes one's face, and combs one's hair, and one sings while washing one's face and combing."

The "He" who "will not take it [the supernatural attractiveness] away" presumably is the Provider. The name and clan are ostensibly not sung, but said.

2.

Now! Listen!
White *Tsugv:tsala:la!*
You rest Above.
You fail in nothing.

Very quickly—Ha!—come speak!
He! Quickly break it up!

(Her name is _____.)

Her soul is not to think of others over there!
Of my body itself alone will this woman be thinking!

Most *di:dagale:n(v)dhoʔdí:yi* are tornadically damaging—to a relationship, and to the individuals who form that
relationship. This one is not injurious. One does not use it
to achieve revenge. It is for deftly snipping the ties that
bind a desired girl to a boy friend against whom the incantator harbors no particular ill will.

Says its label: "To draw away a woman with. This
which is written is to break up easily with." The text is
merely to be said the standard four times.

The incantation is from *Gwagwó:hi.*

3.

Now! Listen!
Red *Dhla:nuwa!*
You rest Above.

Ha! Very quickly You have just descended.

Ha, then! You fail in nothing.

Ha! I will be attired like the Red Woman!

This *i:gawé:sdi* is for the same purpose as the preceding example: to break up a love affair, to capture for oneself the female involved in it, and to leave her lover bereft but uninjured. Its source is stated in Part I, No. 12. A statement appended to it informs one as to its utility: "To 'remake' tobacco if you want someone's woman. When one begins, one says what the great crested flycatcher says: '*Ghuwi?! Ghuwi?! Ghuwi?! Ghuwi?.*'" At the end of the text is the direction to insert one's name and clan affiliation.

Why the *Dhla:nuwa* is called upon and another bird is imitated is not obvious to us. The "Red Woman" is fire. The Cherokees think of the sun as a feminine being—thus fire is also a "woman."

4.
(1)

Now! Listen!
Ha! Sea Gull!
You and I are together, the one atop the other.
You and I are attired as one.
You and I are not lonely in the Seven Clan Districts.

Their souls will be going in and out of their bodies.
One single Pathway has just come to lie before them.
They will certainly not be able to turn back.

And now this has just come to befall them.

(2)

And also, Red *Tsugv:tsala:la* from Above!
Let them live somewhere that they will be unable to climb
   over You and me.

You and I are Great Wizards.
You and I are not lonely.
You and I are very bold.

(3)

Ha! Rock!

You and I are still saying to all of you in the Seven Clan
    Districts that You and I have taken their souls from
    their bodies.

You and I have just descended upon them, so that they will
    be unable to think.

And now, one assumes, this has just come to befall them:
    —————, and —————.

(4)

And also, Ancient White One!

Ya:! Now very quickly You have just come to hear.

Yes! Quickly You and I have just elevated the White To-
    bacco to Your Resting-place and mine.

Ha! You and I have just come to make their souls lonely
    with its Smoke.

Truly they are not to find this out.

Now, one assumes, this has just come to befall them.

Although this *i:gawé:sdi* is of greater than ordinary
length, unquestionably it must be delivered for four times,
and more than likely for four mornings. Its form is as unusual as its length.

‹‹

Each of the four spiritual Forces that labors on behalf of its petitioner performs a definite task: the Sea Gull sets and seals the destiny of the doomed mates; the Red *Tsugv:-tsala:la* renders their protective powers impotent; the Rock crushes out their will to resist; the Ancient White one, a ceremonial circumlocution for the Provider, infuses the tobacco with the authority to rob stealthily the couple of its connubial bliss.

The line, "You and I are together, the one atop the other," contains a Cherokee verb-form for which nothing in English would seem to be even an approximate equivalent. The Cherokee implies that the avian spirit and the incantator are in somewhat the same relationship to each other as would be, let us say, two blankets, one under the other, lying upon a bed. There exists stratification, but also continuous mobile contact. In Cherokee the whole sentence is contained in one word.

In the original language, "Their souls will be going in and out of their bodies" is a stunningly effective verbal image of indecision and uneasiness. Like ghostly larvae that burrow in and out, the souls no longer live in the bodies of the bewitched pair; they infest them.

This incantation from *Gha:hl(i)se:ts(i) Tso:dalv* is, says its recorder: "To 'remake' tobacco to separate them in order to take one of them away."

5.

Now! You Brown Man!
The Brown Tobacco has just come to cudgel!

You Black Man!
The Black Tobacco has just come to cudgel!

>>>

Over there the Very Ugly One washes her face in dog
    excrement.

Move away from there!
She is very ugly!

One gets the impression that formerly there may have
existed in North Carolina a rather sizable corpus of *idi:-
gawé:sdi* for the purpose of making a girl unattractive to
men (Mooney and Olbrechts, *The Swimmer Manuscript*,
p. 155):

> This is the kind of incantation which is recited by a medicine
> man at the request either of a scorned lover or a jealous rival.
> In the first case the patron orders the formula [*i:gawé:sdi*]
> to be directed against the haughty object of his affections, and
> tries to make her so loathsome that she who spurned him will in
> turn be scorned by others.

Oklahoma examples of this type of incantation are ex-
ceedingly rare. This specimen from *Tse:gí:i* is captioned:
"Where the woman sits. To prepare tobacco." Apparently
"Where the Woman Sits" is the title of this incantation.

The "Brown Man" is the spirit of tobacco in its normal
state; the "Black Man" is the spirit of tobacco "remade" for
an unpleasant or evil use.

6.

That One over there!
They all are to think that she is very ugly, the woman who
    sits there against dog excrement.

That One over there!
She washes her face in dog excrement.

That One over there!
Move away, man!

A very ugly woman sits nearby!

The identification upon this incantation from *Gha:-hl(i)se:ts(i) Tso:dalv*, a cognate of the preceding *i:gawé:sdi*, states: "This is to turn one back with. To make an unpleasant man or woman lonely." If directed against a man instead of a woman, appropriate substitutions of words must be made.

7.
(1)

This is what my clan is:_____.

Wi:hiyo?! Hiyo?!
Wi:hiyo?! Hiyo?!
Wi:hiyo?! Hiyo?!
Wi:hiyo?! Hiyo?!

This is what your name is: _____.

I will change you into a mere dog.
On the Pathways you will be right behind me, yelping:
"*Wi:hiyo?! Hiyo?!*"

(2)

Wi:hiyo?! Hiyo?!
Wi:hiyo?! Hiyo?!
Wi:hiyo?! Hiyo?!
Wi:hiyo?! Hiyo?!

Your name is _____.
Your people are _____.

I will change you into a mere deer.
On the Pathways you will be right behind me, whimpering:
   "Wi:hiyo?! Hiyo?!"

(3)

Sayi:!
Sayi:!
Sayi:!
Sayi:!

These are your people: _____.

I will change you into a mere sparrow hawk.
On the Pathways you will be right behind me, screaming:
   "Gi:ya! Gi:ya!"

(4)

Wi:hiyo?! Hiyo?!
Wi:hiyo?! Hiyo?!
Wi:hiyo?! Hiyo?!
Wi:hiyo?! Hiyo?!

I will change you into a mere barred owl.
On the Pathways you will be right behind me, hooting:
   "U:wa! U:wa! U:wa! U:wa!"

Not only is this incantation of extraordinary length, but it must be delivered four times. The exertion is doubtlessly worth the trouble; for it is: "For a woman, when she is angry. One whoops upon finishing. One uses her name when finishing."

"*Wi:hiyoʔ! Hiyoʔ!*" seemingly is a dog bark. It may be sung. Whooping at the termination of a ritual is a motive that is relatively infrequent in magic, viewed broadly; it is exceedingly rare in erotic magic.

This *i:gawé:sdi* is a collation of two versions of the text, both of which are from the vicinity of *Gha:hl(i)se:ts(i) Tso:dalv*.

8.

Now! You woman!
I am as beautiful as the *Tsugv:tsala:la*.
I am as beautiful as the Redheaded Woodpecker.
I am as beautiful as the Bluebird.

You Red One!
He bought it from all of you!

Ha! Sparrow Hawk!
All of you bought it with the Red Tobacco Smoke.

Ha, now! This Blue Smoke has just come to divide all of you.

In all things one is not to fail.

Now! Now one assumes that the Blue Smoke has just come to shake the souls of them that you bought.

This I bought!
(Your name is _____, and your people are _____,
   you woman!)

"If they want a woman of yours. To 'remake' tobacco"
is declared to be the purpose of the above *i:gawé:sdi*—in
other words, it is a counter to magic such as is projected by
Nos. 2 and 3.

"You Red [victorious] One!" says the incantator to himself. "He [the incantator] bought it [male attractiveness]
from all of you [rivals]!" Then he points out that all the
charms of his rivals were come by through witchcraft: "All
of you bought it with the Red Tobacco Smoke." Finally, his
superior magic overcomes the wiles of his enemies, and he
is able to say to the woman, "This I bought!"

Although this imaginative charm was written down at
Gwagwó:hi, we suspect that it actually came from *Nv:wo:-
dhi*, in Sequoyah County.

                              9.

Now! Listen!
Quickly Red Tobacco!
You and I have just come to remake the Brown Tobacco.

You and I have just come to place it upon the Cloth.

Quickly, Great Crested Flycatcher!
He and I have just come to bring you the Brown Tobacco.

Your footprints are not to go astray!

   This incantation is from the library of an elderly,

kindly traditionalist who is probably the most revered Cherokee medicine man now living. Its purpose is: "To prepare tobacco to make a mate stay when she [or he] desires to leave. One follows in the direction in which the person went and smokes four times as she [or he] leaves. For a woman or a man."

The *a:hnuwo,* the Cloth, is a transfer from Cherokee medicine. Originally it was a piece of finely dressed deerskin, but for generations cloth has been used. It is a propitiary gift from the patient to the shaman. Botanicals are gathered in it, and it is used in healing ceremonies.

SPIRITS REFERRED TO BY NAME

SPIRITS REFERRED TO BY NAME

1. *Age:hyv Gu:gv* (or *Gu:ga*): I-5; III-17; V-1.
2. Ancient One (Provider): I-19; VII-4.
3. Ants: VI-3.
4. Barred Owl: II-4; VI-7.
5. Bird (unspecified): III-10.
6. Black Man (Tobacco): VII-5.
7. Bluebird: I-22, 23; III-9; IV-5; VII-8.
8. Brown Man (Tobacco): VII-5.
9. Cardinal: III-8, 12; VI-11.
10. Carolina Wren: I-1.
11. Cat: I-19.
12. Cock: IV-2.
13. *Dhla:nuwa:* I-7, 14, 18, 22; II-4, 5; III-4, 6, 7, 8; VII-3.
14. Diamondback Rattlesnake: VI-2.
15. *Di:sdi:* I-23; III-14.
16. Dog: I-6, 8, 9; II-4; V-4; VI-13.
17. Eagle: II-4, 5; VI-8.
18. Fire: I-19.
19. Fishinghawk: III-7.
20. Fog: I-16.
21. Goldfinch: IV-5.
22. Great Crested Flycatcher: I-12, 13; VII-9.
23. Hawk (unspecified): I-15.
24. Hummingbird: III-6, 9, 16.
25. Kingbird: I-12, 13.
26. Lightning: I-16.

27. Little Man: I-21, 24; III-4; IV-4.
28. Little Men: I-8, 9; VI-4.
29. Long-eared Owl: II-4, 5.
30. Meadowlark: III-15.
31. Mourning Dove: I-18; II-6; VI-6.
32. Night: II-6; VI-8.
33. Panther: I-16; VI-10.
34. Pipe: I-20.
35. Provider: II-6; III-13; V-2.
36. Purple Martin: I-23.
37. Rainbow: III-5; V-9.
38. Raven: I-14; II-5, 6; VI-9.
39. Redheaded Woodpecker: I-22; VII-8.
40. Red Man: IV-2; VI-1.
41. Red Woman (Fire): VII-3.
42. Rock: VII-4.
43. Scarlet Tanager: III-6, 8.
44. Sea Gull: II-2, 6; III-9; VII-4.
45. Seven Thunderers: VI-1.
46. Snapping Turtle: VI-4.
47. Sparrow Hawk: III-9; IV-5; VI-5, 6, 7; VII-8.
48. Spider: I-19, 21; II-3; V-12.
49. Sun: II-6; III-4.
50. Tobacco (or Tobacco Smoke): I-8, 12, 13, 14, 16, 20, 21, 22, 23; II-5, 6, 7; III-7; IV-4; VI-5, 9, 11, 12, 13; VII-4, 8, 9.
51. Tobacco Moth: II-7.
52. *Tsugv:tsala:la:* I-22, 23; III-4, 5, 6; IV-2, 5; V-12; VII-2, 4, 8.
53. Two Men: VI-12.
54. Velvettail Rattlesnake: VI-2, 10.

55. Whippoorwill: II-1.
56. Wild Goose: II-2, 7.
57. Wolf: I-16.
58. Yellow Mockingbird: I-4, 7; II-7; III-9; IV-4.

BIBLIOGRAPHY

BIBLIOGRAPHY

ASTROV, MARGOT, Editor
    1962. American Indian Prose and Poetry: An Anthology. Capricorn Books. New York, N.Y.
GILBERT, WILLIAM HARLEN, JR.
    1943. The Eastern Cherokees. Anthropological Papers no. 23, Bureau of American Ethnology, Bulletin 133, pp. 169-413. Washington, D.C.
KILPATRICK, JACK FREDERICK
    1962. The Sìquanìd' Dìl'tidégi Collection. Sacred Formulas of the Western Cherokees, series 1, no. 1. Bridwell Library Publications no. 2. Southern Methodist University. Dallas, Texas.
    1962. An Etymological Note on the Tribal Name of the Cherokees and Certain Place and Proper Names Derived from Cherokee. Journal of the Graduate Research Center, vol. 30, no. 1, pp. 37-41. Southern Methodist University Press. Dallas, Texas.
KILPATRICK, JACK FREDERICK, and KILPATRICK, ANNA GRITTS
    1964. Cherokee Burn Conjurations. Journal of the Graduate Research Center, vol. 33, no. 1, pp. 17-21. Southern Methodist University Press. Dallas, Texas.
    1964. Friends of Thunder: Folktales of the Oklahoma Cherokees. Southern Methodist University Press. Dallas, Texas.

163

MOONEY, JAMES

    1891. Sacred Formulas of the Cherokees. Seventh An-
        nual Report, Bureau of American Ethnology, pp.
        307-97. Washington, D.C.

    1900. The Cherokee River Cult. Journal of American
        Folklore, vol. 13, pp. 1-10.

    1900. Myths of the Cherokee. Nineteenth Annual Re-
        port, pt. 1, Bureau of American Ethnology, pp.
        3-576. Washington, D.C.

MOONEY, JAMES, and OLBRECHTS, FRANS M.

    1932. The Swimmer Manuscript. Bureau of American
        Ethnology, Bulletin 99. Washington, D.C.

SWANTON, JOHN R.

    1929. Myths and Tales of the Southeastern Indians.
        Bureau of American Ethnology, Bulletin 88.
        Washington, D.C.

WITTHOFT, JOHN

    1946. Bird Lore of the Eastern Cherokees. Journal of
        the Washington Academy of Sciences, vol. 36,
        no. 11, pp. 372-84.

WITTHOFT, JOHN, and HADLOCK, WENDELL S.

    1946. Cherokee-Iroquois Little People. Journal of
        American Folklore, vol. 59, pp. 413-22.